THE COMPLETE BEGINNER'S GUIDE TO AI

Your Easy Guide to Artificial Intelligence, Real World Applications, Ethical Issues, and Future Innovations

GLORIA LEMBO

D1519900

CONTENTS

INTRODUCTION

Your morning begins with a gentle melody orchestrated by your AI assistant, which analyzes your sleep patterns and knows the right moment to wake you—no jarring clang of an old alarm clock required. In the kitchen, your coffee automatically begins brewing as your daily schedule, optimized for your first meeting, illuminates the smart display in your kitchen. News updates tailored to your interests play in the background as you prepare for your day. This incredible image of technology integrated into daily living isn't a glimpse into a distant future; it's the reality of today, powered by artificial intelligence.

AI is more than a tech fad growing more popular by the day. It represents a significant part of modern life, and its influence is only set to increase. Did you know that more than 85% of Americans are already using AI everyday (Johnson 2023). From AI integrations in smartphones to voice assistants and ride-sharing apps, AI's role in our lives is deepening, making a basic understanding of the technology more necessary than ever.

The Complete Beginner's Guide to AI is here to clear the fog surrounding artificial intelligence. AI can often seem confusing or scary at a glance, but this book is crafted for people like you—those curious about how AI technologies are developed, deployed, and dictated by ethical considerations, without all of the jargon and super techy stuff getting in the way. We'll explore how the digital brains of AI influence sectors from healthcare to finance, debunking popular myths and addressing common fears along the way.

I'm thrilled to guide you through the captivating world of AI, a journey powered by my fascination with how technology can reshape our world. My mission is simple: to make AI accessible and understandable for you. This book isn't about coding or complex algorithms—it's about understanding how AI can transform how we live and work, as well as how you can harness its benefits.

The best part about this book is that it requires no prior knowledge of AI. All you need is curiosity and a willingness to engage with the material. Together, we'll peel back the complexity surrounding artificial intelligence, shifting it from a daunting subject into an intriguing part of your everyday life.

UNDERSTANDING AI FUNDAMENTALS

As your days unfold, the invisible guidance of AI-driven technology shapes much of what you experience, often without a second thought from you. AI itself is based on many different fundamental concepts that can seem complicated at a glance, but with a closer look, become rather simple. This chapter is your guide to understanding the fundamentals of artificial intelligence, breaking down its components, operations, and its pervasive role in our everyday lives.

WHAT IS ARTIFICIAL INTELLIGENCE? CLEARING THE AIR

Artificial Intelligence, or AI, may sound like a high-tech term reserved for scientists or engineers, but it's something you interact with more often than you might think. At its core, AI is the science of making machines smart and enabling them to perform tasks that typically require human intelligence. These tasks include learning, reasoning, problem-solving, under-standing language, and recognizing patterns. AI manifests in various forms, from the simple algorithms that recommend what video to watch next on YouTube to more complex systems like autonomous vehicles navigating traffic. The scope of AI is vast and often intertwined with everyday technologies, making it integral to the modern conveniences we know and love.

Think about the voice assistant on your smartphone or smart home device. Whether it's Siri, Alexa, or Google Assistant, these AI-driven systems make use of natural language processing to understand your questions and commands, and machine learning to improve their responses over time based on your interactions. There's also customer service, where the chatbots that handle your inquiries on websites are powered by AI algorithms that interpret and learn from vast arrays of data to provide instant responses that are increasingly accurate and helpful. Predictive text, another common AI feature, anticipates what you might type next in your text messages based on your language patterns and everyday usage.

Understanding how AI operates can seem overwhelming, but it's quite similar to how a chef perfects a recipe over time. Just as a chef might adjust the seasoning, change the cooking time, or try different techniques to improve a dish based on feedback from diners, AI systems continuously improve by learning from new data and experiences, refining their models to become more accurate and efficient. This capability to learn and adapt sets AI apart from traditional programmed systems and is a core component of its operations.

Looking into the future, the potential developments of AI are limitless. We are on the brink of more advanced AI integrated into personalized healthcare, where AI could predict diseases from medical imaging faster and more accurately than human doctors.

In public safety, AI could manage smart cities, optimizing everything from traffic patterns to energy use, reducing costs, and increasing efficiency. The innovations on the horizon promise to enhance the capabilities of machines while offering new opportunities for human creativity and ingenuity.

THE EVOLUTION OF AI: A BRIEF HISTORY

The roots of AI stretch back to the mid-20th century and the visionary insights of Alan Turing, who is often hailed as the father of modern computer science. Turing proposed the question, "Can machines think?" which sparked decades of inquiry and innovation. His 1950 paper introduced what is now known as the Turing Test, which set the stage for the modern pursuit of creating machines that could mimic human thinking processes. In 1956, John McCarthy coined the phrase "Artificial Intelligence" during the Dartmouth Conference, putting a name to the field's ambitions (Anyoha 2017). From these theoretical beginnings, AI has evolved from simple programmed machines to complex systems capable of learning and adapting.

Among the significant milestones that took AI from concept to reality was the development of the "Perceptron" program in 1958 by Frank Rosenblatt (Banoula 2023). This early form of a neural network was a precursor to the algorithms driving many of today's AI applications. Rosenblatt's work attempted to model how the human brain processes information and lay foundational ideas that would become central to AI research.

However, the real surge in AI capabilities came much later with the advent of big data and increases in computational power. Data became the new oil in the 1990s and early 2000s, fueling AI systems with vast information needed to learn and make decisions. This era also saw the development of deep learning techniques that significantly improved the accuracy and functionality of AI systems, enabling more complex applications such as autonomous vehicles and sophisticated voice recognition systems.

Generative AI, particularly in its modern form that leverages deep learning techniques, has been developed by various researchers and teams over recent decades, making significant strides in the process. One significant milestone was the development of Generative Adversarial Networks (GANs) by Ian Goodfellow and his colleagues in 2014 (Giles 2018). GANs are a framework for training neural networks to generate new content, such as images. For example, GANs can be used to generate realistic-looking photos of people who don't actually exist or to create artwork that resembles a specific style. This breakthrough marked a significant advancement in the field of generative AI, enabling the creation of original content like images, music, and text. Generative AI models, such as ChatGPT, now represent a new frontier in AI's capabilities, pushing the boundaries of what machines can understand and generate.

AI research has not remained confined to purely technical or computational problems, but has also expanded into numerous fields, influencing virtually every domain of inquiry and industry. In healthcare, AI now assists in diagnosing diseases with greater accuracy than ever before. In environmental science, it helps model climate change scenarios and optimizes energy consumption in large-scale systems. Each application models AI's versatility and capacity to contribute meaningfully to pressing global challenges. Moreover, AI research methodologies have evolved, with a growing emphasis on interdisciplinary approaches, combining insights from data science, psychology, linguistics, and ethics to craft systems that are intelligent, socially aware, and responsible.

In modern times, public perception of AI has experienced its own evolution. Initially, AI was viewed with curiosity and skepticism, with many people concerned about its impact. The portrayal of AI in media and literature often leaned toward scenarios of dystopian futures dominated by intelligent machines, which did no favors in comforting people about the integration of AI in daily life. However, as practical applications of AI have become more ingrained in everyday life, the focus has shifted toward a more nuanced understanding of AI's role as a tool that, when used wisely, enhances our abilities and skills rather than replaces them. Discussions around AI now address ethical considerations, focusing on issues such as privacy, bias, and the future of employment in an increasingly automated world. These discussions attempt to soothe concerns regarding AI use and responsible integration by recognizing both the positive and negative impacts of such tools.

DECODING AI, MACHINE LEARNING, DEEP LEARNING, AND GENERATIVE AI: WHAT'S THE DIFFERENCE?

AI, machine learning, deep learning, and generative AI are four terms that are often used interchangeably, which leads to confusion about their unique role. They are fundamental to understanding the current world of today's technology; therefore, understanding how these terms connect and differ is critical.

Let's start with an analogy. Imagine learning a new language.

- **Artificial Intelligence (AI)** is like a language school that offers various courses (e.g., French, Spanish, Chinese). It covers a wide range of topics.
- **Machine Learning (ML)** is like your personalized language tutor who adapts the teaching method based on your progress. It fine-tunes your learning experience.
- **Deep Learning (DL)** is like mastering complex grammar rules or pronunciation nuances. It dives deep into specific language aspects.
- **Generative AI** is when you start composing original poems or stories in that language - creating something new.

With this understanding in mind, we can now take a look at how these terms and technologies differ in a practical sense.

AI is the umbrella term for machine learning and deep learning. It encompasses all programming that allows machines to mimic human cognitive functions like learning and problem-solving. For example, personal assistants like Siri and Alexa utilize AI to perform various tasks, from setting reminders to answering questions. This is based on both machine learning and deep learning principles.

Machine Learning is a subset of AI, and it refers to algorithms that enable computers to learn from and make predictions based on data. Machine learning comes into play with applications like Netflix or Amazon's recommendation systems, which predict what you might want to watch or buy next based on your past browsing history on those platforms.

Deep Learning is a subset of machine learning. It uses layered (hence "deep") neural networks to analyze various data factors. These layers enable the system to understand and learn from vast amounts of unstructured data. Deep learning is at work in more complex tasks, such as facial recognition technologies used by Facebook to tag photos or by smartphones for security.

Finally, there is Generative AI—a type of technology within deep learning that can generate new content like text, images, audio, and code based on what users like you ask for. For example, ChatGPT is a model that can chat with you in natural language by answering questions and coming up with creative replies. Another example is DALL-E2, which specializes in creating digital art from scratch.

In each of these examples, the systems rely on a significant amount of data, learning from each interaction to improve their accuracy and functionality.

As these models become more sophisticated, they expand the potential for AI to be applied in solving complex, real-world problems. For example, in healthcare, deep learning algorithms can now analyze medical images with accuracy that matches or surpasses that of human experts, leading to faster and more accurate diagnoses that can then be actioned by skilled human professionals. In the automotive industry, deep learning is essential for developing autonomous systems that enable self-driving cars to "see" and navigate their surroundings. These technologies push the envelope on what machines can do and as these technologies continue to evolve and intersect, they promise to transform every corner of our lives, making our interactions with machines more intuitive, efficient, and increasingly indispensable.

EXPLORING THE BUILDING BLOCKS: ALGORITHMS AND DATASETS

Taking a deeper look at AI, there are two key building blocks that create the foundation for artificial intelligence: algorithms and datasets. Understanding how algorithms and datasets function together will give you a clearer picture of how AI operates as a whole.

Algorithms

Algorithms are the backbone of AI. They provide the necessary framework against which machines can make decisions and solve problems. An algorithm is essentially a set of rules or instructions designed to perform a task or solve a problem. These rules guide the AI systems in processing data and making decisions, much like a recipe guides a chef through the steps of preparing a dish. The complexity of these algorithms can vary greatly, from simple instructions that handle basic tasks to intricate systems capable of learning and adapting from data over time.

Algorithms are categorized into several types, each suited to different tasks and functions within the realm of AI. Among the most fundamental are supervised and unsupervised learning algorithms (Google, n.d.):

- **Supervised Learning Algorithms:** These are trained on a pre-labeled dataset, which means they learn to predict outcomes based on the input data they're given. For instance, they could be trained to recognize photos of cats by being fed thousands of images already labeled as "cat" or "not cat." This type of learning is similar to teaching a child with flashcards; once that child learns what each card represents, they can identify the same objects elsewhere.

- **Unsupervised Learning Algorithms:** These are used when the data has no labels, and the system being trained has to find patterns and relationships within the data on its own. These algorithms are particularly useful for segmenting data groups in complex datasets, like categorizing customers based on their purchasing behavior without prior information about them. This method can be thought of as giving a child a set of blocks of different shapes and colors and letting them organize the blocks into groups without being told how to categorize them.

Data

Just like we as humans learn through experience, AI has to experience something in order to make connections and come to an understanding of our world. This is where data comes into play. We learn over time, experiencing a wide array of events over our lifetimes, and AI's version of this is analyzing and processing datasets.

In other words, data is the fuel for AI; it powers the learning algorithms central to AI systems, which is what enables them to make predictions and decisions. For example, recommendation systems used by streaming services like Netflix or Spotify analyze data from millions of users to learn patterns in viewing or listening behavior. These systems use such patterns to predict what new movies or songs a user might like, personalizing the content to the user's taste and enhancing user experience as a result.

However, the quality and diversity of the data being used are critical. High-quality, diverse data ensures that AI systems learn more effectively and make more accurate predictions. Poor quality or biased data, on the other hand, can lead to skewed or unfair outcomes, such as a facial recognition system that fails to accurately identify individuals from certain demographic groups because it was not trained on a diverse enough dataset. Hence, significant effort is put into collecting, cleaning, and preparing data before it is used to train AI systems in order to avoid these pitfalls. This process includes removing errors, handling missing values, and ensuring that the data represents real-world scenarios where the AI will operate.

Quality data represents the focal point around which reliable and effective AI systems are built. As such, data scientists spend considerable amounts of time preprocessing data to improve its quality, which involves normalization, transformation, and feature extraction techniques. These techniques aid in shaping the raw data into a format that AI algorithms can work with effectively, thus enhancing the overall performance of the AI system.

Some Preprocessing Techniques	Examples
Data Cleaning: handle missing values	A dataset of student grades might have some missing scores. You can replace these missing values with the average score of the class for effective interpretation.
Data Cleaning: remove duplicate values	If a customer dataset has duplicate entries for the same customer, removing these duplicates ensures accurate customer counts.
Data Cleaning: fix typos or inconsistent data formats	In a dataset of birthdates, you can ensure all dates follow the same format (i.e., YYYY-MM-DD).

Some Preprocessing Techniques	Examples
Data Normalization: adjust values to a common scale	In a dataset of calorie counts based on different serving sizes, you can normalize the calorie content to the same serving size. Normalizing the serving size can help you accurately compare their calorie content.
Data Transformation: aggregate data	In a dataset of daily sales volume, you can aggregate the data to monthly sales to analyze the data at a higher level.
Data Transformation: encode data	Many machine learning algorithms require numerical input. In a dataset that contains car colors ("Red," "Blue," "Green") the text is converted to a numerical value (Red = 1; Blue = 2; Green = 3).
Feature Extraction: create new features	In a dataset of birth dates, you can create a new feature for "age."

Understanding these foundational elements of AI—algorithms and data—creates a clearer picture of how artificial intelligence functions and evolves. Through these building blocks, AI systems gain the capability to perform a wide array of tasks, from driving cars to providing personalized recommendations, and continue to grow more sophisticated with each iteration. As we advance further into the AI age, the evolution of these algorithms and the optimization of data processes will play key roles in shaping the future of this field.

NEURAL NETWORKS EXPLAINED: MIMICKING HUMAN BRAIN FUNCTIONS

Think about the vast network of neurons and synapses in our brains. These aspects of our biology form an intricate web of connections responsible for everything, from our thoughts to our emotions and every decision we make. Neural networks in artificial intelligence are inspired by this complex architecture of the human brain. They are designed to simulate the ability to learn and interpret the world around us. At its core, a neural network is a series of algorithms that endeavors to recognize underlying relationships in a data set through a process that mimics how the human brain operates.

To break it down, a neural network is composed of layers of interconnected nodes, or neurons, each linked by synapses. These nodes are not unlike the neurons in our brain. In a basic neural network, there are three primary layers (Ognjanovski 2019):

- the input layer, where data enters the network
- the hidden layer, where the data is processed
- the output layer, where the result is delivered.

Each neuron in these layers processes the input it receives and passes on its output to the next layer. The connections between these neurons carry "weights" that adjust as the network learns, affecting how strongly a neuron influences another.

The learning process of neural networks is fascinating and centers around adjusting these weights based on the data they process, a method known as backpropagation. In backpropagation, the network makes a prediction, measures how accurate the prediction is, and then flows back through the network to adjust the weights. This adjustment helps the network improve its predictions in future iterations. For example, if a neural network is tasked with identifying animals in photographs, and it incorrectly labels a cat as a dog, the error is propagated back through the network's layers. This feedback adjusts the weights, which increases the likelihood of correct classification in future attempts.

Neural networks come in various forms, each suited to different tasks. Each type of network offers a specialized approach to learning and interpreting data, making them invaluable tools in the AI toolkit (Great Learning Team 2024):

- **Convolutional Neural Networks (CNNs):** These are exceptional at processing visual data. They are commonly used in image recognition software, as they can work to identify faces, landscapes, and objects in photos accurately.
- **Recurrent Neural Networks (RNNs):** These are better suited for sequential data like text or speech. They can predict the next character in a sequence, making them ideal for language translation applications or voice recognition systems.

Neural networks are not without their challenges and limitations. One of the most significant is the amount of data required to train them effectively. Neural networks learn from examples, and the fewer examples they have, the less accurately they can infer and generalize from that data. This requirement for large volumes of data can make training neural networks resource-intensive.

Another challenge is their "black box" nature, referring to the difficulty in deciphering how they come to specific conclusions. This opacity can be problematic, especially in applications where understanding the decision-making process is imperative, such as in healthcare diagnostics or autonomous driving. These challenges highlight the complexities of designing and implementing neural networks, pushing researchers and developers to continually innovate and refine these systems to enhance their reliability and transparency.

NLP UNPACKED: HOW MACHINES UNDERSTAND US

Natural language processing, or NLP, bridges human communication and machine understanding, representing an incredible aspect of artificial intelligence where machines are taught to interpret, understand, and even generate human language. NLP involves the application of algorithms to identify and extract the natural language rules we use in our own communication. This means that unstructured language data can be converted into a form of language that computers can understand.

The importance of NLP rests in its ability to foster seamless interactions between humans and machines—ones that enhance user experience and extend the capabilities of machines to perform tasks traditionally requiring human intelligence, such as translating languages, responding to voice commands, and summarizing large volumes of text.

A diverse set of techniques are employed within NLP, each serving a unique function in language processing (ProjectPro 2024):

- **Tokenization:** a technique where text is broken down into individual words or phrases called tokens. This process is crucial because it helps structure the data for further analysis, like understanding the frequency and arrangement of words.
- **Part-of-Speech (POS) Tagging:** a process where each word in a sentence is marked with its corresponding part of speech, such as noun, verb, adjective, and so on. This

helps machines understand the grammatical structure and meaning of a sentence.

- **Sentiment Analysis:** a key technique that involves analyzing text to determine its sentiment, whether positive, negative, or neutral. Companies often use this method to monitor and analyze customer reviews and social media comments to gauge public sentiment about their products or services.
- **Machine Translation:** a technique used by tools like Google Translate that allows for the automatic translation of text from one language to another. It leverages massive datasets and complex algorithms to provide quick and increasingly accurate translations for efficient communication.

Applications of NLP are increasingly ubiquitous, finding their way into various aspects of everyday life and business operations. Chatbots and virtual assistants like Siri, Alexa, and Google Assistant, for example, work with NLP to interact with users in a conversational way. These pieces of software, through NLP, are able to understand and process human speech to perform a wide range of tasks—from setting alarms to providing weather updates. In customer service, NLP makes way for chatbots to respond instantly to inquiries, significantly improving efficiency and customer satisfaction. These are just a couple of the wide-ranging applications of NLP in bringing more convenience to our modern lives.

Despite its advances, NLP still faces significant challenges that stem primarily from the complexities and nuances of human language. Understanding context, for instance, can still be tricky for AI software, even with the help of NLP. This is because the meaning of words can drastically change based on the context in which they are used. Sarcasm and irony add layers of complexity that can lead to misinterpretations by NLP systems, which can struggle to discern the intended tone and meaning behind such expressions. Cultural nuances also create challenges for NLP-based software because different cultures may use the same words in different ways, or convey meaning through subtleties that are difficult for algorithms to detect.

More sophisticated models are needed to meet these needs, which is part of the ongoing research behind NLP today. As NLP continues to evolve, it promises even more seamless and intuitive interactions between humans and machines. The ongoing research and development in this field are geared toward creating systems that understand and generate language more efficiently and do so in a way that is as nuanced and sophisticated as our communication between others and ourselves.

UNDERSTANDING COMPUTER VISION: SEEING AS HUMANS DO

A common question that comes up when considering AI that creates art or uses visual data is how AI is able to see without eyes. Computer vision is an aspect of artificial intelligence that creates ways for computers to interpret and understand the visual world around them, even without having the same biological mechanisms that allow us to do the same. This technology aims to mimic human vision capabilities so that machines can easily identify and process objects in images and videos just as we do. The goal is ambitious: to provide machines with the ability to understand visual information from the environment, which can then be used for specific tasks such as recognizing faces, detecting objects, or analyzing video content.

Fundamentally, computer vision uses algorithms that process visual information. These algorithms analyze the pixels of images and videos to detect patterns corresponding to particular objects, faces, scenes, or actions. This process begins with the input of visual data, which is then processed through various layers of the algorithm, each designed to identify different image elements. For instance, the initial layers might detect simple features like edges and colors. Then, deeper layers work to identify more complex features, such as shapes or specific objects. This hierarchical processing mimics human vision, where simple visual inputs are compiled and interpreted to form a comprehensive understanding of the scene at hand. In other words, computer vision is much like our vision in that it considers a broad overview of an image before delving into the details of each aspect of that image.

The applications of computer vision are quickly becoming more intertwined with our daily lives as these technologies progress. There are countless examples of how these advancements are shaping our daily lives:

- **Social media and personal devices often make use of computer vision.** The facial recognition technology used to unlock your device is powered by computer vision, which analyzes specific facial features to verify your identity securely. Similarly, social media platforms use computer vision to automatically tag photos with your friends' names by recognizing their faces.
- **Computer vision is also helpful in areas like healthcare, where it plays a critical role in diagnostic imaging.** By analyzing images from X-rays, CT scans, or MRIs, computer vision systems can help radiologists

detect abnormalities such as tumors or fractures more quickly and accurately.

- **Augmented reality (AR) is another area where computer vision is deeply relied upon.** AR applications overlay digital information onto the real world, enhancing what you see by merging it with interactive, virtual elements. For example, AR can be used in educational settings to create immersive learning experiences that visualize complex academic concepts in real time to enhance students' understanding and engagement.

- **In the automotive industry, self-driving vehicle technology relies heavily on computer vision to navigate safely.** These vehicles use cameras and sensors to interpret their surroundings, detect road signs, and avoid obstacles, paving the way toward safer and more efficient transport systems.

With such advancements, it's only natural for concerns regarding privacy, security, and ethical issues to arise. As facial recognition is deployed more widely, it raises questions about surveillance and the right to privacy. Using computer vision in surveillance systems can deter crime and enhance public safety, but it also creates the potential for misuse if not appropriately regulated. Moreover, as self-autonomous technologies become more common, they could reshape industries and economies, influencing everything from job markets to urban planning. As AI continues to develop, each of these considerations is being carefully considered.

RECAPPING AI JARGON: KEY TERMS TO KNOW

Learning about artificial intelligence is like learning a new language. The terms can seem confusing at first, but as you continue to understand AI and related technologies, that fog begins to lift. To help you feel more at home with AI discussions and enable you to engage with more confidence, this section recaps some of the essential AI terminology covered throughout the course of this chapter.

AI: AI, or Artificial Intelligence, is a branch of computer science that enables machines to perform tasks that typically require human intelligence. By processing large amounts of data and using algorithms to identify patterns, make decisions, or predict outcomes, AI systems can learn and improve over time. This learning process allows AI to adapt to new information and situations, making it capable of handling complex tasks like language translation, image recognition, and even autonomous driving.

Algorithm: Algorithm is a term that sits at the heart of AI. An algorithm is simply a set of instructions designed to perform a specific task. It's quite similar to a recipe, where each step guides you to the desired outcome. In a practical sense, your smartphone makes use of algorithms to decide the order of posts you see in your social media feed based on your past interactions, thus leading to apps that are more likely to show you content you will enjoy. This adaptive capability of algorithms to learn from your behavior and adjust the content accordingly models the ever-changing nature of AI in everyday applications.

Data: Data is the fuel that powers the learning algorithms. Datasets are collections of structured information that can include anything from text, images, and audio to numerical data, all labeled or categorized to provide context for the AI to learn from. The quality and diversity of a dataset are crucial, as they directly influence the accuracy and effectiveness of the AI's performance.

Machine Learning: Machine learning is a subset of AI that teaches computers to learn from data and improve their performance over time without being explicitly programmed for every task. For instance, email platforms use machine learning to filter out spam. They analyze incoming messages and learn to distinguish between spam and legitimate mail based on various indicators—such as sender information, keywords, and user interactions with similar emails. This continuous learning process allows the system to adapt and effectively filter spam as tactics evolve, all thanks to machine learning.

Deep Learning: Deep learning dives even deeper, functioning as a specialized subset of machine learning. It involves multi-layered neural networks that analyze large amounts of data to identify patterns and make decisions. For example, Netflix employs massive data banks in order to bring you the best user experience each time you open the platform. Deep learning algorithms process user preferences, viewing habits, and even minute interactions to recommend movies and TV shows with astonishing accuracy. This capability is not just limited to entertainment; deep learning is also helpful in medical diagnosis, where it can help detect anomalies in medical images, potentially leading to early detection of diseases such as cancer.

Generative AI: Generative AI is becoming more and more popular thanks to its focus on creating new content rather than simply analyzing data. This branch of AI involves models that generate text, images, music, and complex simulations. For example,

ChatGPT, a natural language model, can produce new and original text based on a few user-entered prompts, aiding in tasks from drafting emails to creating detailed reports. Similarly, DALL-E, another AI model is used to create realistic images that range from realistic scenes to surreal and imaginative artwork, showcasing the potential of AI in creative fields such as art, design, and visual storytelling.

Neural Networks: Neural networks are another vital aspect of AI, inspired by the human brain's architecture. These networks are collections of algorithms that identify underlying relationships in data through a process that mimics how neurons signal each other in the brain. A familiar application of neural networks is in digital personal assistants like Amazon's Alexa or Apple's Siri. These assistants process your voice commands by deciphering your words and intent through neural networks and then fetching information or performing actions based on your requests. The ability of these systems to understand and respond to a diverse array of commands in real time is a direct result of the complex neural networks operating behind the scenes.

Natural Language Processing: Lastly, natural language processing (NLP) is an AI technique that enables computers to understand and process human language. An everyday example of NLP is the translation features in apps like Google Translate. Whether trying to decipher a menu in a foreign language or translate a webpage, NLP algorithms analyze the text and convert it into your native language while maintaining as much of the original meaning as possible. These algorithms are required to navigate the complexities of human language, from varying sentence structures to idioms and slang, in order to meet these goals. This serves to highlight the sophisticated capabilities of NLP in bridging language barriers.

For those eager to explore these concepts further, many low-cost and free resources are available online. Platforms like Coursera and Khan Academy offer courses specifically tailored to beginners, covering everything from the basics of algorithms to more advanced topics in machine learning and neural networks. Engaging with these resources can deepen your understanding and appreciation of AI, all while empowering you to participate more actively in conversations about how this technology shapes our world.

As you become more familiar with these terms and see how they manifest in the technology you use daily, the once-daunting world of AI becomes more approachable. The language of AI is increasingly becoming the language of our future. Each aspect of AI that you learn about and understand adds to your ability to navigate this new technological frontier.

AI IN EVERYDAY LIFE

In an increasingly digital age, your interaction with the world is not curated by chance; rather, algorithms come into play time and time again to predict and influence your choices. Every day, as you scroll through your social media feeds, you're engaging with an advanced form of artificial intelligence that tailors your digital environment to your personal tastes and habits.

In this way, AI makes your world, both online and offline, more streamlined to your needs and passions. In this chapter, we will explore how AI can seamlessly integrate into your daily rituals and core considerations that coincide with that integration.

HOW AI CURATES YOUR SOCIAL MEDIA FEEDS

Every time you hit the "like" button on a post, watch a video, or even pause to look at a picture on social media, AI is learning about your preferences. This data feeds the personalization algorithms that social media platforms use to curate your feed, ultimately leading to more engaging and enjoyable content showing up on your timeline. These algorithms are driven by artificial intelligence and are designed to analyze patterns in your behavior to predict what kind of content you will find to be valuable or engaging. Essentially, they create a unique digital profile based on your interactions and use this profile to influence what you see every time you open up your favorite social media apps.

However, these algorithms don't just bring you content that aligns with your proven interests. They also improve your experience online by introducing new topics and perspectives that broaden your experience and engagement on the platform. This balance is important because it avoids isolating you from diverse viewpoints and new experiences while keeping your interests at heart all the while. AI developers constantly tweak their algorithms to find an ideal mix of new content and familiar, interest-based posts that maximize your engagement without creating a repetitive social media atmosphere.

In the midst of these technological advancements, ethical considerations arise. Many people hold justified concerns regarding privacy and personal data use. Because AI systems require vast amounts of data to learn and make accurate predictions, this necessity raises privacy concerns, as the data often includes personal information that users might not intend to share widely. Therefore, ethical AI use requires transparent data handling practices, user consent prior to data collection, and robust security measures to protect your stored data.

As you scroll through your social media feeds, remember that behind every post, like, and share, there is a complex system of AI at work. This system is designed to learn from and adapt to your preferences, providing a tailored digital experience that reflects your interests and behaviors. Understanding how AI shapes these experiences allows you to engage with social media more knowingly and critically so that you can maintain control over your digital landscape.

Reflective Exercise

Take a moment to reflect on your social media use:

- Think about the last few pieces of content that you interacted with on your social media feed. What do these elements reveal about your interests?
- Consider how diverse the content you encounter is. Are you seeing a variety of perspectives, or does it feel limited?
- Reflect on your privacy settings. Are you comfortable with the information you're sharing?

Reflecting on these questions can help you become more aware of your digital footprint and AI's role in shaping your social media experience.

SMART ASSISTANTS: HOW SIRI AND ALEXA KNOW ALL

Imagine you're cooking dinner. Your hands are covered in flour and other ingredients, but you need to set a timer for the oven immediately. Instead of stopping what you're doing, washing your hands, drying your hands, and setting that timer manually, you simply call out to your smart assistant, "Hey Siri, set a timer for 20 minutes," and it's done. This convenience is made possible by voice recognition technology, an integral aspect of today's smart assistants like Siri, Alexa, and Google Assistant. These devices use a combination of advanced microphone technology and complex software algorithms to recognize your voice and understand your commands.

The process of these assistants being able to help you begins with the device's microphone picking up your voice and converting the sound into a digital signal that such software can interpret. This signal is then analyzed by AI algorithms that sift through various databases of language and syntax patterns to understand what your command truly means. These databases are built from countless examples of spoken language, granting your device the ability to comprehend your unique accent, syntax, and phrasing to help you out.

The technology that powers these interactions is known as natural language understanding (NLU), which not only recognizes speech but interprets the intent behind your words. This capability allows smart assistants to handle various requests, ranging from answering questions about the weather to controlling smart home devices and many features in between. NLU is so effective due to its ability to parse language, determine the structure and meaning of your sentences, and help your smart assistant respond naturally and intuitively. This interaction seeks to truly understand your words in context, a complex process that AI manages through deep learning models that mimic human neural networks.

Smart assistants are becoming a major part of managing daily tasks for many people. They are convenient for everyone, whether you want a hands-free technology experience or need certain accommodations to be able to thrive. Such assistants can sync with digital calendars, set reminders, control smart appliances, and even help manage your emails. Imagine telling your device to preheat the oven before you get home or to adjust your house's thermostat—all possible with a few spoken commands. This tech-powdered "magic" saves time and allows for multitasking, where you can handle other activities without pausing to type or manually fumble with buttons to set devices a certain way. AI can even make daily chores more enjoyable, even if they can't complete all of those tasks for you directly. For example, while doing laundry—something AI isn't quite ready to handle—you can ask your assistant to read the latest news or play your favorite podcast, keeping you happy and engaged without stopping your flow of chores and responsibilities.

The functionality of smart assistants hinges directly on their ability to process and use your personal data in meaningful ways. These devices constantly learn from the data they collect each time you interact with them and refine their algorithms to understand your preferences and speech patterns better. While this data processing absolutely has benefits, it also comes with concerns about privacy—how is your data being protected? Fortunately, your data protection is just as important to the people implementing these programs as it is to you. Companies behind intelligent assistants implement various data security measures to address these concerns. Encrypted data storage, secure internet connections, and privacy controls that let you manage your data are standard and part of all reputable software. You can review what data is stored and delete history if needed, providing a level of transparency and control over your information that reduces privacy concerns.

Looking ahead, the future of smart assistant technology is on track to become even more integrated and proactive. This future involves making life easier and making the interaction with technology more natural and intuitive through a deeper under-standing of user needs and preferences. Anticipated developments in this field center around more nuanced conversations where assistants remember past interactions and anticipate needs based on your schedules and habits. For example, suppose you have a meeting every Tuesday. In that case, your assistant might proactively remind you of the meeting or suggest the best time to leave home to beat the traffic without having to be prompted to do so. Further integration with other smart devices and services is also expected, leading to a more interconnected home where your assistant knows about your schedule and pref-erences and those of other household members—optimizing household routines and enhancing life's conveniences resultantly.

AI IN YOUR SHOPPING EXPERIENCE: ONLINE AND IN-STORE INNOVATIONS

When you shop online, have you ever noticed how the website knows exactly what you're looking for? Or, after browsing a few products, you start seeing recommendations that feel like they were handpicked for you. This isn't just a coincidence; it's artifi-cial intelligence in action. AI uses your past purchase data and browsing history to create a personalized shopping experience tailored just for you. It analyzes the patterns in your previous interactions—what you've bought, what you've searched for, and even what you've lingered on—to predict what you might like and present those options to you. This makes your shopping experience more relevant and significantly more convenient as it saves you time by directing you to items you are more likely to purchase.

Moreover, AI's role in personalizing your experience extends to optimizing the user interface—the actual application or website you're browsing. Depending on your shopping habits and preferences, the layout of the website or app might adjust to highlight products or categories that interest you most. For example, if you frequently purchase books from an online store, AI might prioritize book recommendations or deals prominently on your homepage. This tailored customization enhances your shopping experience and increases the likelihood that you'll purchase products you love, benefiting both you and the retailer.

AI's influence continues to reshape the retail landscape of physical stores as well. One of the innovations that stands out the most is the integration of AI technologies like smart mirrors and interactive displays. These tools use AI to improve your shopping experience by providing personalized recommendations and information. For example, smart mirrors in clothing stores can suggest other items to complement the outfit you're trying on, show you how a piece of clothing would look in a different color, or even allow you to share the image with friends for instant feedback. Interactive displays can provide detailed product information and reviews when you pick up an item, making it easier to make informed choices.

But AI's role isn't just customer-facing; it's also revolutionizing how stores manage their inventory and logistics. AI systems can be used to analyze sales data, predict trends, and help retailers understand what products are hot and which ones are not. This data-driven approach means that stores can keep just the right amount of stock on hand, reducing excess inventory and minimizing waste. Additionally, AI optimizes logistics by predicting the best routes for delivery trucks, determining optimal delivery schedules, and even forecasting potential disruptions in the supply chain. These capabilities ensure that products are restocked efficiently and remain available to you and other people who frequent those shops.

However, while these innovations have amazing benefits, there are also concerns that arise, particularly surrounding data privacy and employment. The amount of personal data collected to fuel these technologies can include everything from purchasing habits to individual preferences, which raises significant privacy issues. Retailers are thus obligated to handle this data responsibly through robust security measures and transparent policies that inform customers about how their information is used. Furthermore, as AI continues to automate more tasks, there is a growing concern over the impact on jobs in the retail sector. While AI can increase efficiency and reduce costs, it also has the potential to displace workers, especially in highly repetitive roles. This shift calls for mindful integration, where the benefits of AI are harnessed to enhance service and efficiency while also considering the social impacts—such as the need for retraining and transitioning the workforce to new roles where they can provide value beyond what AI can achieve.

PERSONALIZED ENTERTAINMENT: AI BEHIND NETFLIX AND SPOTIFY

In daily life, AI also factors into entertainment. When you settle in for an evening of streaming your favorite show or unwinding with some music, the choices presented to you are far from random. They result from intricate AI systems designed to streamline media content to your unique tastes. Content recommendation systems drive this personalization. These complex algorithms analyze your viewing and listening habits to predict what you might enjoy next, based both on your own data and the data of others who share your favorite shows or tracks. Such systems track the choices you make—the shows you watch, the songs you play, and even the content you skip—to compile a detailed profile of your preferences. With this data, AI algorithms identify patterns that might not be immediately apparent but reveal your underlying tastes and preferences ("Maximizing Engagement with AI Personalization: Strategies for the Modern Marketer" 2024).

This process involves more than simply analyzing the genres or artists you prefer and placing that content on your screen. It dives deeper to consider factors like the time of day you watch certain types of content, the devices you use, and how your viewing habits change over the week or year. For instance, you might prefer watching action-packed movies on Friday nights on your TV but opt for light-hearted comedies on your tablet during weekday commutes. AI uses this multifaceted insight to curate a list of suggestions tailored just for you so that the content resonates on a personal level. Another example of this is Spotify's Daylist feature, which provides you with a customized playlist for not just your taste, but for the time and day of the week as well.

Beyond just recommending content, AI is valuable for optimizing the user interface and features of platforms like Netflix and Spotify so that your interactions can be as enjoyable and efficient as possible. AI tests different layouts and functionalities in what is known as A/B testing, where two versions of a page are compared to see which performs better in user engagement and satisfaction. This method allows developers to fine-tune every aspect of your experience, from the placement of the search bar to how content is categorized and presented (Rawat 2017). Such optimizations might seem minor, but they significantly affect how easily you can navigate the platform and find what you're looking for.

AI's influence also shows up within the realm of content creation itself in how music, videos, and other forms of media are produced. In the music industry, AI tools are used to compose music or generate unique sounds, assisting artists in exploring new creative territories. Video platforms use AI to edit and enhance footage, automate subtitles, and even help script video content. These tools augment the creative process so that artists and creators can express their ideas and tell their stories more effectively. While the center of creativity remains distinctly human, AI acts as an influential collaborator by offering tools and insights that can inspire new artistic visions and bring them to life more efficiently.

At the same time, the reliance on AI for content recommendation and creation has challenges and limitations. One significant concern, for example, is the potential for creating echo chambers or filter bubbles, where the system continuously feeds you content that aligns with your existing beliefs and preferences. This phenomenon can limit cultural and intellectual diversity, reinforcing existing biases and reducing the certainty of discovering content that could broaden your horizons. AI is striving to make this less frequent as algorithms become more effective, but it's simultaneously important to be an active participant in critiquing the media you see and searching for diverse perspectives. Moreover, while AI is proficient at identifying patterns and making predictions based on data, it sometimes struggles to fully comprehend the complexities of human taste. The subjective nature of entertainment means that two people with similar viewing histories might react differently to the same content. This nuance can be challenging for AI to capture fully.

SMART HOMES: LIVING IN A CONNECTED WORLD

Let's re-envision your morning for a second. Imagine waking up not to the shrill sound of an alarm but to personalized alarm tones that gently bring you out of your slumber. At the same time, your thermostat adjusts to your preferred morning temperature for optimal comfort, rather than you scrambling first thing in the morning to be comfortable when you wake up. Once a futuristic dream, this scenario is now possible by integrating artificial intelligence with Internet of Things (IoT) devices in home automation systems. AI in home automation takes mere convenience and aligns it with adaptable and personalized environments that foster your ideal lifestyle. They improve energy efficiency and save you time by learning your habits and preferences to manage everything from heating and lighting to security and energy use without you having to lift a finger.

Interconnectivity and system management drive these smart home systems. Through IoT technology, various devices in your home—thermostats, lights, security cameras, and refrigerators just to name a few—can communicate with each other via the internet. This network of devices creates a system that can manage itself to operate more efficiently. For example, your smart thermostat can adjust the temperature when it senses that you've left the house, or your smart locks can activate once your security system is armed. This communication means that your home operates as a cohesive unit, automatically adjusting to your life's rhythms and routines, rather than as a series of separate units that you might stress over or forget about.

User-controlled customization is another significant benefit of AI in home automation. Through user-friendly apps, you can set preferences and schedules that tell your smart devices exactly how and when to perform their tasks. Want the curtains drawn and coffee ready the moment you wake up? Or would you prefer lights that dim gradually as you prepare for bed? All these settings can be customized to suit your preferences thanks to AI's integration in home automation. This ability to modify your home's functionality to your needs improves your comfort. It can even result in better financial management, as optimization settings can lower utility bills through automatic adjustments.

Of course, security and privacy issues can come up when we think about home automation. As homes become more connected, they also become more vulnerable to hacking and breaches. Each smart device can create a potential entry point for cyberattacks, which could compromise your personal information or allow unauthorized control over your home systems. Fortunately, this is something that has been accounted for when it comes to the development of these systems. To counter these threats, it's necessary to secure your smart home devices by using strong, unique passwords, keeping your software up to date (so that the latest and safest updates are always running), and employing network security measures like firewalls and encrypted connections to keep your devices accessible to you and you alone.

Smart homes promise incredible and revolutionary advancements as time goes on. Emerging developments in AI and IoT technology may suggest that homes will become more responsive, efficient, and capable of anticipating needs before you even articulate them. Future smart homes might automatically order groceries when your fridge is empty, suggest recipes based on what's available, or even detect potential maintenance issues before they become serious problems. Innovations like these could transform our living spaces from passive structures to active participants in our daily lives.

AI IN NAVIGATION AND TRANSPORTATION: MORE THAN JUST MAPS

At one point, navigation meant trying to walk a busy path or plan a journey using an incredible amount of human (and error-prone) judgment alongside a good old physical map. This made navigation a struggle. Paper maps, and even the first versions of digital maps and GPS, fall short of accounting for traffic patterns, road closures, and even faster routes that would get you to where you're going in less time.

Today, AI has dramatically transformed how we navigate and manage transportation, making trips more efficient and less fraught with the perils of now-antiquated navigation methods. AI algorithms now have the power to analyze vast traffic data and driver behavior to recommend the best travel routes, highlight routes to avoid, and overall provide recommendations for driving that help your navigation double in efficiency. This analysis is more than picking out the shortest path; it involves predicting traffic congestion and road conditions, and even incorporating real-time incidents like accidents or roadworks into route planning. For example, when you enter a destination into your GPS navigation app, AI algorithms calculate the fastest route based on current traffic conditions, drawing from data collected from thousands of other users on the road. This system continuously updates, recalculating the route as new data comes in to be certain that you always have the most efficient path available.

Outside of maps, AI is also changing the game when it comes to the act of driving itself. Autonomous vehicles, often referred to as self-driving cars or driverless cars, are vehicles equipped with advanced sensors, cameras, radar, and AI software that help them navigate and operate without human intervention. These vehicles use real-time data processing and decision-making algorithms to perceive their environment, interpret road conditions, detect obstacles, and navigate routes safely to their destination (Lutkevich 2019).

The development of self-driving cars is one of the most exciting and futuristic applications of AI in transportation. Based on the information these cars can parse, AI makes split-second decisions on steering, speed, and route adjustments to ensure safe and efficient travel. The intricacies of making these vehicles as reliable as human drivers, if not more so, are immense. They have to understand basic traffic rules and adapt to unpredictable elements such as sudden weather changes or erratic driver behavior from others on the road. All of these elements converge in creating a world where travel is no longer a time-consuming burden. Hours spent in traffic become convenient and productive when an AI-powered car allows you to relax comfortably in the passenger or back seat.

Public transit systems also benefit greatly from AI. Urban centers, where public transportation is often the focal point of the city's mobility, leverage AI to improve the efficiency and reliability of their transportation services. AI applications in public transportation often incorporate predictive maintenance for vehicles and scheduling that shifts with human activity, among other features. Predictive maintenance uses AI to analyze data from various sensors in buses and trains to predict when a component might fail. Transit authorities can reduce downtime and maintenance costs by addressing these issues before they lead to breakdowns, resulting in more reliable service thanks to AI (Kawano 2024). Shifting schedules, on the other hand, can adjust transit schedules in real-time based on various factors like passenger demand, traffic conditions, and service disruptions. As a result, resources are used optimally, wait times are reduced, and overcrowding becomes a thing of the past.

Even the environment sustains benefits because of AI's integration into transportation. AI's ability to optimize route planning and vehicle operations has the potential to significantly reduce fuel consumption and, by extension, carbon emissions (Conrad 2024). In autonomous vehicles, AI-driven optimization of driving patterns and speeds can lead to more fuel-efficient travel and a lower carbon footprint. Also, public transit systems that use AI for scheduling and maintenance make public transport a more appealing option for commuters due to increased efficiency, which can potentially reduce the number of private vehicles on the road and their overall environmental impact.

FITNESS AND HEALTH TRACKING: THE INVISIBLE AI COACH

Our daily lives also stand to improve thanks to AI integrations in fitness and health tracking. In an age where personal well-being is being emphasized more and more, artificial intelligence has many benefits when it comes to improving our health and fitness routines. AI-powered wearable technology, for example, has revolutionized how we monitor and understand our bodies by turning everyday activities into opportunities for health insights. These wearables, ranging from fitness bands to smartwatches, are equipped with sensors that track many forms of physiological data, including heart rate, sleep patterns, and physical activity levels. This constant monitoring gives you a comprehensive picture of your health throughout the day, unlike intermittent checks at the gym or in a doctor's office. As a result, you can feel empowered to take charge of your well-being in novel ways.

The real magic of AI in health begins with the interpretation of this physiological data. AI algorithms analyze the information collected to identify patterns and trends over time. For instance, monitoring your heart rate and activity levels can help AI gauge your fitness level and how it responds to different workouts. Sleep tracking, another tool many AI-powered health devices offer, can be used to assess the quality of your sleep based on movements and heart rate variability throughout the night. This data helps you understand what factors might affect your sleep, such as stress or physical activity, allowing you to make informed decisions to improve your sleep quality thanks to the hard work of AI.

AI doesn't just track your health and fitness data; it personalizes your fitness journey. When AI is able to take a look at your performance data and personal goals, its algorithms can create fitness programs that align with your objectives and adapt to your progress as it changes. These personalized programs adjust their intensity and duration based on how your body responds and what can help you harness the most health benefits (TechAhead 2024). For example, suppose that AI notices you're achieving a particular fitness goal faster than expected. In that case, it might suggest more challenging exercises or increase the frequency of workouts to keep you engaged and improving. Conversely, if you're struggling with a particular aspect of your fitness regimen, AI might scale back the intensity to prevent burnout or injury.

Predictive health tracking is another area where AI is making a big difference. AI can identify potential health issues before they become serious by analyzing trends and data over time. For example, certain devices can detect irregularities in your heart rate or a consistent downward trend in your physical activity. AI algorithms can flag these changes for further investigation, which can lead to taking control of your personal health and intervening before medical issues are irreversible. This early detection is key in preventive healthcare, as it allows for timely medical intervention to mitigate more severe health issues. AI's ability to analyze data on a granular level—often noticing subtleties that might be overlooked in a traditional healthcare setting—proves its capability as a preventive tool that offers a layer of health monitoring that is both continuous and non-intrusive.

AI in fitness and health tracking is also slowly becoming more integrated alongside healthcare providers and how they treat our health on a regular basis. The data collected by your AI-powered devices can be invaluable for your healthcare providers because it gives them a more detailed view of your health and habits. With your consent, this data can be shared with your doctors, who can use it to tailor your medical treatments more precisely. For instance, your physical activity and heart rate information can help your doctor customize cardiovascular treatment plans or lifestyle recommendations specifically suited to your needs. This integration enriches the quality of healthcare you receive.

In our daily lives, AI is only set to become more integrated. While many people worry about the implications that this can have for our privacy and security, it's clear that AI offers benefits that will only improve over time. From streamlining your entertainment to keeping you in good physical health, AI's algorithms and capabilities mean that it can keep an eye on your life and automate certain processes, freeing you up to focus on aspects of your life that aren't possible to be automated—like having fun!

AI IN THE PROFESSIONAL WORLD: TRANSFORMING INDUSTRIES

Think about a hospital powered by AI. You walk into the building and within minutes—not hours—AI has analyzed your medical data with a precision and analysis unmatched by human doctors. From there, your human doctor can take a look at the data and work with you to form AI-inspired treatment plans known to target your symptoms efficiently. By the end of your visit, not only are you confident that your care is in the right hands but you are already feeling better because of the revolutionary treatments that AI allows for.

This is the real-world impact of artificial intelligence in healthcare today. AI's integration into various industries revolutionizes how professionals approach problems, make decisions, and improve outcomes. In healthcare, these innovations are particularly influential, offering new ways to diagnose, treat, and care for patients with efficiency and precision that were unthinkable just decades ago.

AI IN HEALTHCARE: DIAGNOSIS AND PATIENT CARE INNOVATIONS

Through AI, we can examine various impacts on the processes involving diagnostics and patient care. AI is driving brand-new innovations that lead to more impactful diagnosis and treatment, all while considering the individual history and needs of each patient.

Enhanced Diagnostic Accuracy

In healthcare, the accuracy of a diagnosis can significantly influence treatment outcomes. AI has the potential to be one of our leading helpers in enhancing diagnostic accuracy, mainly because of its ability to interpret medical imaging. Advanced AI algorithms are now being used to analyze and identify patterns in images from X-rays, CT scans, and MRIs—ones that may be invisible to the human eye. For example, in radiology, AI can detect subtle signs of diseases such as cancer at much earlier stages, often before patients exhibit symptoms. These algorithms are trained on thousands, sometimes millions, of images, and learn from each to improve their diagnostic precision. The speed of AI analysis also means that diagnosis can happen in real time, reducing the anxious wait times for patients and allowing for quicker initiation of treatment.

Personalized Medicine

One of the most promising aspects of AI in healthcare is its ability to personalize treatment. Every patient is unique, not just in their DNA but in their lifestyles, environments, and medical histories. AI algorithms excel at sifting through large amounts of data, such as genetic information, to create treatments specific to individual patients. This approach, known as personalized or precision medicine, allows for the customization of healthcare, with treatments and medications optimized for each individual's genetic makeup. Personalized medicine aims to increase the efficacy of treatments while minimizing side effects—leading to better patient outcomes and more efficient healthcare delivery.

Robot-Assisted Surgery

Surgical robots, guided by AI, are changing the future of surgical operations as we know them. These robots combine real-time data from patient medical records with precision instrument control, which makes way for surgeries that are less invasive and more accurate than those performed exclusively by human hands. The use of AI in surgery extends—not replaces—the capabilities of surgeons. This leads to shorter recovery times and less postoperative pain for patients. Furthermore, robot-assisted surgery can access areas that might be challenging for human hands, resulting in the potential for new types of surgeries that were not previously feasible.

Patient Monitoring and Care

AI's impact extends beyond diagnosis and surgery and into ongoing patient care. AI-powered tools and devices can monitor patient vitals and conditions continuously, not just within hospital settings but also at home. As a result, a seamless approach to health management can be created without the gaps common to previous monitoring habits. This constant monitoring allows for real-time adjustments in treatment, immediate alerts in case of emergencies, and better management of chronic diseases as well.

Incorporating AI into healthcare redefines the relationship between patients and health services. As AI continues to advance, the precision of medical care can be furthered, inefficiencies can be reduced, and, most importantly, your health can be sustained by professionals taking care of you.

AI IN FINANCE: RISK ASSESSMENT AND FRAUD PREVENTION

The stakes are incredibly high when it comes to money management, and the room for error is minimal. Artificial intelligence has extended itself into the world of financial operations, shifting how we consider finances. From how we assess risks to managing and preventing fraud, AI's ability to analyze vast amounts of financial data rapidly and precisely improves financial outcomes both for businesses and individuals alike.

Predictive Risk Assessment

For investors and financial managers, the primary goal is to maximize returns while minimizing risks. AI models can help with this. AI has the ability to predict risks with remarkable accuracy by sifting through and analyzing patterns from extensive financial data. This capability means that banks, investment firms, and individual investors can make more informed financial decisions. For instance, AI algorithms can evaluate market conditions, track stock performance trends, and monitor economic indicators to forecast market volatility. This information can then lead to strategic investment decisions, such as when to buy or sell assets, which industries are safer investments during economic downturns, or when a market is likely to be bullish or bearish. Leveraging AI in risk assessment means that financial entities can safeguard investments and identify potential high-return opportunities that might not be obvious to even the most seasoned financial analysts.

Fraud Detection Systems

The risk of financial fraud is large in a world where digital transactions are the most common way money travels. AI steps into this digital money market with powerful fraud detection systems that are quickly changing how businesses and consumers like you protect their financial assets. These systems employ machine learning algorithms to monitor and analyze transaction patterns in a non-stop way for clear and up-to-date information. They are trained to detect anomalies that could indicate fraudulent activities, such as unusually large transactions, rapid frequency of transactions in an account, or suspicious international payments (DigitalOcean 2023). For example, if someone tries to make a high-value purchase in a country they've never visited before, AI systems can flag this transaction in real time and prompt immediate verification steps to confirm the transaction's legitimacy. This proactive approach means that financial fraud can begin to become a thing of the past, all while you and I appreciate strong financial peace of mind.

Automated Trading

High-frequency trading (HFT) is a form of stock exchange, and AI is impacting this financial area, too. AI algorithms execute large volumes of orders at very high speeds—a process that humans cannot match in speed and efficiency. Because these algorithms analyze market data to execute trades at optimal prices and times, they capitalize on small price fluctuations that occur within fractions of a second. The precision and speed of AI-driven automated trading enhance market efficiency and increase liquidity, which is beneficial for the overall stability of financial markets (Chen 2019). This automation also means that traders and institutions can achieve better pricing, reduce the cost of trading, and improve the execution of their transactions, ultimately leading to more robust and responsive financial markets.

Credit Scoring

We all know about our credit scores, those little numbers that show lenders how much they can trust us. Being able to access lines of credit is important for individuals and businesses alike, and AI is changing how even long-standing norms like credit scores operate. Traditional credit scoring methods often rely on a limited set of criteria, which can exclude potential borrowers who may be creditworthy but lack an extensive credit history. AI is positively disrupting this aspect of finance by incorporating a wider range of data points to assess creditworthiness.

For example, alternative data such as utility bills, rental payment histories, and even social media behavior can be analyzed by AI algorithms, which can then provide a more comprehensive assessment of a person's reliability as a borrower. It might sound small, but this broader approach to credit scoring means that access to loans and financial services is more widely available to people working to obtain financial support for homes, education, and businesses. AI's inclusivity in credit scoring has significant benefits for financial equity and stimulates economic growth by widening the pool of individuals and companies that can access capital.

AI IN MARKETING: TARGETING AND ANALYTICS

When you scroll through your social media feed and see an ad that seems like it was made just for you, or when you receive an email promotion that perfectly matches your interests, it's not just luck—it's artificial intelligence working behind the scenes. AI has completely changed the marketing game by providing tools that allow for better targeting and analytics than ever before. These technologies allow marketers to cut through the noise and deliver content that resonates personally with you as an individual, which is helpful for you as a consumer and for businesses.

Precision Targeting

Precision targeting is perhaps one of the most significant advances brought by AI in marketing. It works by analyzing data collected from various consumer interactions online—including browsing habits, purchase history, social media activity, and even geographic locations—so that AI algorithms can identify specific audience segments likely to be interested in particular products or services. For example, if you're more likely to be interested in makeup than cars, AI can extract this from your browsing and purchase history to show you products that you really care about. This personal touch means that the internet is more productive and enjoyable for you.

Precision targeting through AI helps marketers direct their campaigns to target individuals so that resources are utilized more efficiently and effectively on people who are interested in specific products or services. For example, if a dataset shows that a particular demographic spends more time on fitness-related content online, a company selling health products can direct its marketing efforts specifically to that group. This level of specificity in targeting increases the likelihood of a sale, of course, but it more importantly means that ads are engaging and non-intrusive for you as a consumer.

Marketing Analytics

In addition to precision targeting, AI has played a massive role in improving marketing analytics capabilities. Traditional analytics can provide surface-level insights such as page views, click rates, and general demographics that are somewhat helpful, but AI takes things a step further. AI-driven analytics dig even deeper, offering insights into customer behavior and preferences at a much more detailed level. These tools use advanced algorithms to track patterns and trends over time, analyze how consumers interact with content, and understand what drives their decisions. Marketers can then use this information to optimize their strategies in real time, such as by adjusting elements like ad placement, content design, and messaging to align more closely with user preferences. This readily changing approach to analytics provides a clearer picture of what works and what doesn't, thus allowing for constant improvements in marketing strategies for greater efficacy as market conditions change.

Personalization at Scale

Personalization at scale is another area where AI shines in marketing. In the past, personalizing content to individual preferences was a resource-intensive process that could only be done to a limited extent. Companies weren't able to really speak to each individual person. Now, however, AI makes it possible to personalize marketing at scale, simultaneously tailoring content to millions of individuals' preferences. Algorithms that analyze individual user data create personalized experiences, from customized email marketing messages to individualized product recommendations on e-commerce sites and everything in between. As a result, this improves customer satisfaction and loyalty while boosting engagement rates, as users are more likely to interact with content that feels specifically designed for them.

Looking Ahead

Taking a look at the future, AI in marketing is gearing up for even more innovative developments. Predictive analytics, for instance, is an area where rapid growth is anticipated. Technologies in predictive analytics use AI to understand past consumer behavior and predict future behaviors and trends based on that data. Marketers can then use these insights to anticipate market shifts and consumer needs and adapt their strategies to stay ahead of the game.

Additionally, as voice search and smart home devices are welcomed into more and more homes, AI will play a major role in optimizing content for voice interactions and integrating marketing strategies with these new platforms. This evolution will open up new channels for reaching consumers, further expanding the impact of AI in marketing.

AI IN MANUFACTURING: AUTOMATION AND EFFICIENCY

Where manufacturing is concerned, efficiency is king. AI is transforming factory floors across the globe, making them smarter, faster, and safer. Integrating AI into manufacturing processes, often called smart manufacturing, brings a new level of intelligence to production lines. Predictive maintenance is a feature that stands out, where AI algorithms predict machinery failures before they occur—similar to what we discussed earlier regarding transportation maintenance. These systems analyze data from sensors on equipment to detect anomalies that might indicate a potential breakdown, allowing maintenance to be conducted before costly, unplanned downtime occurs. Real-time adjustments are another benefit, where AI systems optimize production parameters on the fly, responding to new data inputs like changes in raw material quality or environmental conditions. This capability maintains the production quality, enhances the speed, and reduces waste—increasing overall efficiency in the process.

Automated Decision Making

Automated decision-making further proves the plus sides of AI in manufacturing. In traditional settings, production planning and inventory management decisions often require human input and are based on periodic reports and analyses. AI changes this dynamic by facilitating automated decision-making based on real-time data for the most up-to-date decision-making processes. For example, AI systems can adjust production schedules based on real-time demand data and supply chain conditions, ensuring that manufacturing output always aligns with market needs without requiring constant human oversight.

Quality Control

Manufacturing quality control has also seen a massive improvement with the adoption of AI. Through high-resolution cameras and advanced image processing algorithms, AI systems inspect products as they move along the production line. These systems are trained to detect defects or inconsistencies with far greater accuracy and speed than human inspectors, saving time and placing human workers in other areas of manufacturing where their input is more valuable. Whether spotting a tiny imperfection in automotive paint or ensuring a microchip is free from manufacturing defects, AI-driven quality control systems maintain high product quality standards (Trident Information Systems 2024). The immediacy of this process means that issues can be addressed as soon as they are detected, which reduces the cost and impact of recalls or rework. For consumers like you and I, this translates into higher confidence in the products they purchase, as it's less likely to grab a defect off the shelf or have a broken product shipped to your door.

Worker Safety

In an industrial setting, worker safety is a top consideration. AI is a top-notch way to ensure that all workers are safe thanks to the development of robotics and safety analytics. AI-powered robots are now common in situations that are too dangerous for human workers, such as handling hazardous materials or performing high-precision tasks in unsafe environments. These robots have sensors and machine learning algorithms that allow them to navigate and manipulate objects with high dexterity and minimal risk. This means that the lives of workers are respected, and their health maintained.

Additionally, AI-driven safety analytics systems can monitor workplace conditions by using data from various sensors to predict and alert about potential safety hazards. For example, if a machine begins to operate outside of its normal functions or restrictions, the system can immediately alert operators or shut down the machine to prevent accidents before they occur. This protects workers and builds up a culture of safety that extends to every level of the organization.

AI IN AGRICULTURE: PRECISION FARMING AND SUSTAINABLE PRACTICES

In the open fields where your food begins its journey to your table, a quiet revolution is taking place, powered by artificial intelligence. AI-driven technologies like drones and advanced sensors are now familiar sights above rows of crops, where they monitor plant health and soil conditions with an accuracy that reframes how farming is done. These tools offer farmers a birds-eye view of their crops and a deep dive into the health of their fields, leading to interventions that are not just timely but precisely targeted.

For example, drones with high-resolution cameras and infrared sensors can detect plant disease before it's visible to the human eye. They analyze images of the crops to identify color changes and heat signatures that indicate stress or disease—shifts that we wouldn't be able to pick up on until the damage has already been done. This monitoring level also helps apply the exact amount of chemicals needed, reduce waste, and prevent the overuse of pesticides and fertilizers that can harm the environment while preserving the hard work of farmers everywhere.

The role of AI involves more than monitoring; it can also actively predict and manage the needs of a farm. Weather prediction is one aspect of this process to which AI contributes significantly. Advanced AI systems have the capacity to analyze weather data and accurately forecast changes, which empowers farmers to make informed decisions about planting, watering, and harvesting. For example, if an AI system predicts a sudden frost, farmers can take measures to protect sensitive crops from damage.

Similarly, AI helps with water management, which is a critical concern in many farming regions. By predicting rainfall patterns and moisture levels in the soil, AI systems can improve irrigation schedules and ensure that crops get the right amount of water at the right time, thus conserving water and reducing costs associated with over-irrigation.

Automated Equipment and Efficiency

The introduction of self-driving tractors and harvesters is another area of agriculture where AI is making a substantial impact. These machines operate with little human input and can run 24/7, significantly reducing the labor costs associated with farming (Max_zero 2023). More importantly, they bring precision to tasks like planting, plowing, and harvesting that minimize damage to crops and reduce resource wastage. For instance, autonomous tractors equipped with GPS and real-time data can adjust planting depth and spacing in immediate response to variations in soil conditions detected by their sensors. This precision ensures that every seed can grow into a healthy plant, optimizing yield and efficiency.

AI IN EDUCATION: PERSONALIZED LEARNING PATHS

AI and education are often thought to be distinct purely because of generative AI misuse. The reality is that AI in education, when used properly, has the ability to personalize and enhance the learning experience of each and every student, both in and outside of the classroom.

Customized Learning Experiences

One of the most significant impacts of AI in education is its ability to customize learning experiences to the individual needs of each student. Think about a classroom where each student receives instruction explicitly formulated to their learning pace and unique style of understanding concepts—incredible, right? AI makes this possible by analyzing data on how students interact with educational materials, identifying patterns in their learning behaviors, and adapting the content accordingly. For instance, if a student excels in visual learning but struggles with text-heavy materials, AI systems can automatically adjust the curriculum to incorporate more visual aids for better student comprehension and retention of information.

This level of personalization is about more than adapting to learning styles, though. AI also incorporates the pace at which a student learns in its analysis, which can reduce time-based inefficiency in the classroom. AI learning tools can provide additional challenges to quick learners or extra support to those who need more time, creating an academic environment where each student is met at their level. Such adaptive learning systems keep students engaged and prevent the common issue of advanced learners feeling bored or under-challenged and less advanced learners feeling overwhelmed.

Automated Administrative Tasks

The administrative burden on educators can often be overwhelming, with substantial time spent on tasks such as grading and taking attendance, which detracts from their primary focus—teaching and interacting with students. AI is changing this aspect of education as well by automating many of these routine tasks. For example, AI systems can automatically grade multiple-choice and fill-in-the-blank tests, providing immediate feedback to students and saving teachers countless hours. More advanced AI applications are even beginning to assess more subjective responses and essays, although these tools are typically used in a supportive role to assist teachers rather than replace their judgment. Moreover, AI can handle attendance through facial recognition software that quickly identifies students as they enter the classroom, instantly updating attendance records so that classes can get started right away.

These forms of AI-based technology simplify administrative processes, enhance record-keeping accuracy, and reduce the likelihood of errors that can affect everything from students' grades to their participation records. By shifting these administrative burdens from teachers to AI systems, educators are freed up to focus more on teaching and personalized interaction with students, ultimately enriching the educational experience and improving outcomes for students.

Interactive Learning Tools

Integrating AI in education also brings about many different interactive learning tools that have the potential to transform traditional learning environments. Virtual labs and simulations powered by AI, for example, provide students in remote or underprivileged areas with hands-on learning experiences that were once only possible in well-equipped educational institutions. These tools simulate complex scientific experiments or mathematical models so that students can safely explore and experiment in a virtual space without a need for expensive lab equipment. For instance, virtual chemistry labs help students combine chemicals and observe reactions with detailed visualizations that mimic real-life experiments, improving their understanding of chemical processes without the equipment or health risks of hazardous materials.

These interactive tools are particularly beneficial in making education more accessible regardless of geographical or social constraints. They supplement traditional learning and often provide a richer, more engaging educational experience.

Performance Tracking and Feedback

There's a lot to love about the role of AI systems in continuously monitoring and assessing student performance. AI software trained for tracking and feedback means that educators and students have access to precise, timely feedback that is imperative for effective learning. These systems track progress over time and analyze both errors and successes, which can then be used to provide personalized feedback that helps students understand their strengths and areas for improvement. For example, AI-driven platforms can identify patterns in a student's responses, pinpointing specific concepts the student has not mastered and providing targeted exercises to address these gaps.

The ongoing assessment opportunities provided by AI lead to a more fruitful experience between students and educators, where feedback is not limited to report cards or scheduled reviews. It is an integral part of daily learning that can help students adjust their learning strategies and engage with content more effectively each minute of every day. For educators, the detailed understandings provided by AI systems into each student's performance make it easier to adjust their teaching strategies to meet the needs of every student in their class.

AI IN THE CREATIVE ARTS: CHANGING THE LANDSCAPE OF ART AND DESIGN

Now, let's shift our focus to the creative arts, where artificial intelligence has begun to create art, designs, and other forms of media using its incredible innovations. For many, the idea of AI in art isn't ideal—they often feel that AI isn't truly able to be creative, catalyzing opinions on AI art drastically. However, AI in these fields is not just about harnessing technology to create new forms of expression, and it's certainly not about displacing human artists; rather, it's about redefining the processes through which creativity is manifested. AI's role as a collaborator rather than just a tool is shining distinctly in the fields of music and visual arts particularly. Artists and musicians are exploring AI-generated music and art, which involves algorithms that can analyze styles and patterns to create unique pieces reminiscent of human-made art. This collaboration opens up many possibilities—such as the ability to experiment with complex patterns and sounds that would be difficult, if not impossible, to achieve independently.

As a practical example, consider how AI algorithms analyze extensive databases of paintings or music already. When these systems do so, they are also learning from different styles and genres to generate new creations. These systems can identify underlying patterns in Gothic architecture, Impressionist paintings, or Baroque music and apply these styles to create brand-new artworks or symphonies. This is just one example of how such capabilities expand the software and tools available to artists. AI also allows for the accessibility of art. For example, someone with a passion for music but without the ability to play an instrument

—be it due to financial constraints, disability, or another reason —can now compose music using AI software that understands and applies complex musical theories and techniques.

Art also encompasses design and architecture. In design and architecture, AI's impact is especially evident in how it hones the ability to simulate outcomes and optimize buildings as a result. Architects and designers can thus work with AI to visualize and test the viability of their ideas in virtual environments before any physical work begins, saving time, labor, and physical resources in the process. AI models can also improve the security and intuitive nature of buildings because they simulate how a building will withstand earthquakes, how it will affect the flow of traffic, or how energy-efficient it is, just to name a few examples. These insights can then be used to refine designs and ensure both functionality and sustainability. Beyond that, AI-driven design tools can generate innovative design alternatives based on specified criteria as a form of assistive brainstorming. These tools help explore a wider array of options quickly, therefore reducing the time and resources typically required for iterative design processes.

The media industry, too, is experiencing a transformation due to AI's ability to assist in content creation and editing. From writing articles to producing movie trailers, AI tools are proving to be invaluable. They can think about viewer engagement and preferences to suggest content adjustments or create promotional materials likely to capture public interest with ease, saving time for human creators to focus on fleshing out ideas of their own without the hassle of marketing. AI-driven software can even edit videos! Such software has the ability to do this by suggesting cuts or transitions, for instance, that improve the narrative flow, or by optimizing content for different platforms

—whether it's a full-length feature for theater release or a short clip for social media. This application of AI streamlines production processes to meet audience expectations, engagement goals, and more.

However, the advent of AI in creative fields in particular also brings about a wide range of ethical considerations that have to be addressed. Issues of originality and copyright are at the forefront of these concerns. When an AI creates a piece of music or a painting, who holds the copyright? Is it the AI creator or the user who inputs the initial parameters, or should it be considered public domain work? These questions are among the many being answered by professionals in related fields.

Furthermore, the role of human artists in an increasingly AI-dominated landscape is a subject of intense discussion. While AI can enhance creativity and open up new possibilities, there is a lot of talk about the unique qualities of human-made art needing to be more valued and preserved. The challenge lies in finding a balance where AI enhances human creativity without overshadowing it, which is a consideration that businesses, individuals, and software developers alike must consider in their work with AI.

AI IN ENVIRONMENTAL CONSERVATION

Conserving the environment—something more important now than ever—hinges on AI showing up as a crucial ally. The ecosystems on Earth are intricate and complex, and their preservation is critical for biodiversity and human survival. While understanding these nuances might be troubling for some humans, AI has the capacity to step in, inform us, and even create direct changes that lead to the preservation of the natural world.

Ecosystem Monitoring

AI's role in monitoring the ecosystems of our planet is increasingly important. The algorithms and sensor-based technologies that AI can power are able to track changes and intervene for wildlife protection when necessary. As AI progresses, for example, we may see the development of satellites with AI systems that can scan the oceans for illegal fishing activities or drones that fly over forests to monitor wildlife populations. These incredible technologies would be formed from the existing efforts of AI to improve nature today, and have the potential to provide conservationists with detailed, real-time data that was once impossible to gather.

AI's capability extends to the microscopic analysis of environmental data as well. For example, in marine conservation, AI algorithms can examine water samples to detect pollutants at incredibly low concentrations that less precise technology can't pick up on. From there, AI focuses on alerting authorities to contamination events almost instantaneously. On land, AI-driven cameras and sensors deployed in wildlife reserves can track animal movements, monitor their health, and even predict poaching events before they occur.

Poaching

Speaking of poaching, AI technologies can truly shift the paradigm when it comes to our ability to fight poaching. Poaching is a persistent threat to wildlife conservation, driven by illegal trade and the demand for animal products. As a result, poachers hunt and kill usually extremely endangered wildlife, taking their population numbers down even further. AI, fortunately, is here to help.

AI-powered surveillance systems deployed in wildlife reserves use motion sensors and night vision capabilities to detect unusual activity. These systems moderate the movements and alert park rangers to immediate threats for quick responses and the protection of wildlife. Additionally, AI is used to predict poaching hotspots based on historical data and live inputs, which means that conservation efforts can be focused where they are most needed. This readily actionable approach to conservation helps sustain the survival of species that might otherwise be driven to extinction (Needhi 2024).

Climate Modeling

Climate modeling is another area where AI is making a splash. Traditional models used to predict weather and climate patterns are limited by the number of variables in climate and their complex interactions. AI shapes improvements in these models by handling large datasets more efficiently and identifying patterns that human analysts might miss. For example, AI systems are used to simulate and predict climate conditions under various global warming scenarios, which helps scientists observe and predict potential future changes in climate patterns. This information is critical for policymakers and communities as they prepare for and adapt to the impacts of climate change, such as rising sea levels, more intense weather events, and shifts in agricultural productivity.

Resource Management

Resource management, particularly regarding water and energy, is yet another aspect of how AI can improve nature. Smart grids driven by AI, for instance, can improve the distribution and use of electricity, therefore reducing waste and increasing efficiency. These systems adjust the energy flow based on demand and supply data that is gathered in the moment, which allows for renewable energy sources like wind and solar to be integrated more effectively. In water-scarce regions, AI algorithms manage irrigation systems to help crops receive the right amount of water at the right time, minimizing waste, and conserving our precious water supplies at the same time.

Professional sectors are benefitting from AI more and more as the days pass. Everything from entertainment to the Earth itself stands to be nurtured by AI's incredible advancements, keeping us safe, happy, healthy, and entertained as a result.

INTERACTING WITH AI: USER EXPERIENCE AND ACCESSIBILITY

So far, we've explored countless areas of AI in daily life. Many of those options involve subtle AI use, where the magic of AI operates without a second thought from us. As AI becomes more and more helpful, it's also important to understand what interacting with AI is going to look like.

Imagine sitting in your living room, speaking a question into the air, and getting a response from your smart speaker with just the right information—or better yet, having a conversation with your car that can adjust its route based on real-time traffic updates while you focus on sipping your coffee. These scenarios are now everyday realities thanks to advances in AI technology, and these interactions are only going to become more profound. This chapter dives into how AI technology evolves and can be interacted with from the lens of a user.

VOICE RECOGNITION AND AI: BEYOND COMMANDS

If you've ever enjoyed the convenience of a "Hey, Siri!" or an "OK, Google!" then you're already familiar with voice recognition and AI. For many people, these technologies represent simple and accessible modes of communicating with AI. However, these technologies are far more than just software capable of understanding basic commands. AI in voice recognition has gone above and beyond and now represents an incredible facet of what it means to interact with AI.

Advanced Voice Recognition Capabilities

Voice recognition technology has traveled a long way from its rudimentary form of recognizing mere words. Today's AI-driven voice recognition systems are adept at deciphering accents, dialects, and even the most subtle nuances of spoken language. If you used voice recognition several years ago, then you'll be able to tell that these advancements have made interaction with AI feel more natural and less robotic. These systems employ refined algorithms trained on vast datasets comprising diverse voice samples to enhance their accuracy and adaptability. This training gives them the opportunity to understand what you're saying and how you're saying it—recognizing mood, tone, and even implied meanings and figurative language. Whether you're asking a casual question about the weather or giving a complex command while driving, AI systems can now process your speech with remarkable accuracy, making interactions smoother and more intuitive.

Interaction Beyond Basic Commands

The evolution of voice recognition technology has brought us to a threshold where AI can engage in meaningful dialogues and assist with tasks beyond basic commands.

Modern AI systems can manage your schedule, help organize your emails, and even offer emotional support in some instances. For example, some advanced AI applications are designed to detect stress or sadness in your voice, responding in supportive and comforting ways, much like a friend or family member would. This capability means that AI can be integral to managing your tasks and supporting your mental and emotional well-being.

Integration with Other Technologies

Voice recognition interfaces are increasingly integrated with other intelligent technologies, creating a user experience that allows technology to mirror daily interactions. In smart homes, voice-activated systems can connect with everything from your refrigerator to your home security system so that you can control your environment with simple voice commands. The integration extends to vehicles as well, where voice recognition allows for hands-free operation of navigation systems, music selection, and even phone calls. This holistic integration of technologies sharpens convenience and improves safety, particularly in driving scenarios, by minimizing distractions.

VISUAL AI INTERFACES: HOW AI USES IMAGES TO INTERACT

As you interact with the digital world, whether flipping through a photo album on your phone, navigating a crowded street via a digital map, or playing an augmented reality game, you are interacting with AI technologies that understand and interpret the visual world. This capability is rooted in what is known as computer vision, which we discussed in Chapter 1. Let's spend a few moments expanding your knowledge of computer vision now.

The process of computer vision begins with the detection of individual objects within an image. This involves recognizing and labeling objects, a task that might seem simple to humans like us but is incredibly complex for machines that lack the biological framework with which to see in a literal sense. Technologies like object recognition are now commonplace in various applications, such as security cameras that can identify intruders and smartphones that unlock with facial recognition instead of a passcode. As you know from Chapter 1, these systems rely on data libraries and models that learn distinctive features of different objects and faces, under various conditions and from different angles, for a fuller understanding of the visual world.

Facial recognition technology, a subset of object recognition, models how AI interprets visual input to perform tasks once thought to be exclusively human. This technology interprets the unique features of a face, such as the distance between the eyes or the shape of the jawline, to identify or verify an individual's identity. This capability is now used in various security applications like airport screening processes and personalized customer experiences in retail environments, where systems can identify returning customers and offer tailored services based on previous interactions ("Understanding Facial Recognition Technology: How It Works and Examples" 2024).

Visual AI interfaces are also able to power AR applications, where digital elements are overlaid on the real world to enhance your interaction with your surroundings. AR apps, for example, can display historical facts over a live camera feed of a landmark, or show how a piece of furniture might look in your living room before you make a purchase. These applications merge real-world visuals with informative or aesthetic digital overlays to create interactive experiences that are both engaging and revealing. Integrating AI-driven visual recognition in AR technologies makes these interactions possible. It ensures they are fluid and responsive, adapting to changes in the environment and user interactions in real time.

Improvements in Accessibility

Visual AI interfaces can also contribute much in the way of accessibility, particularly for people with visual impairments. Technologies that describe visual scenes or identify objects can make daily experiences more engaging and simple for the visually impaired. For example, smartphone apps with AI-powered cameras can audibly describe what they see, such as reading text on a street sign or menu or helping with navigation in complex public spaces. These tools act as visual interpreters by providing descriptions necessary for understanding and interacting with the surroundings.

Also, real-time object identification can help people with visual impairments perform tasks independently, leading to greater confidence and autonomy thanks to the ability to navigate unfamiliar environments. By recognizing and labeling objects around them, these AI systems provide audio cues about their environment, such as warning about a step down on a staircase or notifying them of a nearby seat in a crowded room.

Challenges and Future Trends

Despite the incredible capabilities of visual AI interfaces, they face many challenges that stem from the inherent limitations of current technology. Issues with lighting, where either too much or too little light can affect visibility, significantly impact the performance of visual recognition systems, for example. Similarly, occlusion, where important parts of an object or scene are blocked from view, can lead to inaccurate or incomplete interpretations by AI systems.

Ongoing developments aim to overcome these challenges by improving the algorithms' ability to interpret complex visual inputs under less-than-ideal conditions. Advances in machine learning models are continually improving the robustness of visual AI systems, enabling them to handle variations in lighting, occlusion, and other environmental factors more effectively. Plus, as the datasets used to train these models grow more extensive and diverse, the systems are becoming better at understanding a wider range of scenes and objects, making them more reliable and effective across various applications.

AI CHATBOTS IN CUSTOMER SERVICE: ARE THEY EFFECTIVE?

AI chatbots have been pivotal in customer service, representing a major shift in how businesses interact with their clients. These AI-driven interfaces are designed to handle a wide variety of customer inquiries and respond to them instantly at any time of the day. This round-the-clock availability means that when you have a pressing question about a product at midnight or need assistance with a service on a holiday, the assistance is just a chat away. Because they can take over routine inquiries, AI chatbots free up human agents to tackle more complex issues and boost the overall efficiency of customer service departments. This shift makes room for businesses to allocate their human resources to tasks requiring empathy, judgment, and deep problem-solving skills—where humans excel over machines.

Numerous studies and data analyses underscore the effectiveness of AI chatbots in enhancing customer service and user satisfaction. Research indicates that chatbots can handle up to 80% of routine questions and tasks, which means that these chatbots have incredible potential when it comes to reducing wait times and improving customer satisfaction (Cherniak 2024). The immediacy with which chatbots respond and the 24/7 availability appeal to the modern consumer, who often seeks instant and convenient solutions, as well. The quality of support offered by chatbots is only elevated when you realize that the intricacies of these AI systems enable them to provide personalized responses by accessing customer data, history, and previous interactions.

One of the most compelling qualities of AI chatbots is their ability to learn and adapt constantly. These systems are built on machine learning algorithms that analyze every interaction to improve accuracy and effectiveness. Each query you pose and every piece of feedback you provide is a learning opportunity for the chatbot. Over time, they become more adept at understanding the nuances of human language and the specific needs of customers. This continual learning process allows chatbots to evolve from simply following scripted responses to offering more helpful and contextually appropriate solutions that benefit the customer experience.

While these changes are overall positive, deploying AI chatbots brings up ethical considerations and the need for transparency. For example, it's important that you can identify and know when you are interacting with a machine rather than a human. This awareness means that you're fully informed because transparency in AI chatbots involves clear communication regarding the identity of the chatbot and the extent of its capabilities. This furthermore aids in safeguarding your data privacy and ensuring the information the chatbot accesses to personalize service is protected and used ethically. As these chatbots become more integrated into customer service processes, maintaining this transparency and ethical awareness becomes crucial to building trust —something each company integrating AI has to keep in mind.

As AI technology continues to advance, the role of AI chatbots in customer service is expected to change, not just in handling more interactions but in their ability to conduct them in increasingly intricate ways. Future developments may, for example, allow chatbots to detect customer emotions and respond appropriately, bridging the gap between human and machine interactions. This progression promises greater efficiency and a deeper, more empathetic approach to customer service that could redefine the standards of customer interactions.

ACCESSIBILITY IN AI: TOOLS FOR THE DISABLED

Artificial intelligence is transforming industries, increasing daily convenience, and also playing a stunning role in improving accessibility for people with disabilities. Technologies such as predictive text and voice-to-text transcription services are prime examples of how AI is being adapted to support diverse needs. Predictive text technology, for instance, helps users with mobility or dexterity impairments by predicting the next word they intend to type, significantly reducing the number of keystrokes needed. In turn, pain, frustration, and isolation common for those with disabilities can be reduced. This technology learns from the individual's typing habits to become more accurate over time.

Voice-to-text transcription is another aspect of AI where accessibility is becoming more and more attainable every day. This technology converts spoken language into written text as those words are being communicated, which provides an essential service for individuals who are deaf or hard of hearing. It allows them to participate in conversations or access spoken content in educational and professional settings without delay—meaning that they can converse back readily or ask questions as the urge arises. Much like Alexa and Siri, these AI systems also have the ability to understand and process diverse speech patterns and accents for accurate transcriptions. They can also differentiate between voices in a conversation, taking clarity and usability another step further in group discussions or meetings.

While these technologies are incredible, the importance of customizable AI interfaces regarding accessibility cannot be overstated. Each individual's needs and preferences can vary widely, making flexibility in technology a crucial factor. AI systems with customizable interfaces address this need by allowing users to adjust settings such as text size, color contrast, and command inputs for increased control over their interaction with technology. This also ensures that these tools can be used more effectively and comfortably. For example, someone with low vision can increase text size and contrast to make reading on a screen easier. On the other hand, someone with limited hand mobility might use voice commands to navigate their device instead of tapping or swiping.

It might seem like AI only makes phones and similar devices more accessible, but the incorporation of AI in assistive devices like prosthetics and wheelchairs is revolutionizing what these accessibility aids can achieve. Modern prosthetics equipped with AI can learn and adapt to the user's movement patterns to make the use of those prosthetics a more natural and intuitive experience. For instance, a prosthetic arm with AI capabilities can analyze the movements of the user's residual limb and the surrounding muscle signals to predict and execute precise movements, such as gripping or pointing. This functionality also enhances the quality of life for amputees by empowering them to perform daily tasks more independently.

Similarly, the AI-powered wheelchairs that are currently being developed offer improved mobility solutions that adapt to a user's environment and needs. These wheelchairs can navigate complex terrains and avoid obstacles all on their own thanks to sensors and real-time data processing. As a result, a higher level of safety and comfort can be achieved. These devices may also go on to include customization features that recognize voice commands or interpret other assistive inputs, such as eye movements or brain waves, to support users with varying levels of mobility (Pizzuto 2024).

Despite these advancements in the making, barriers still exist that prevent the full accessibility of AI technologies. One major challenge is the design of AI systems that fully consider the wide range of disabilities. Often, technologies are developed with a one-size-fits-all approach, which can overlook the specific needs of people with disabilities. This might mean that prototypes appear promising for some but immensely out of reach for others. Additionally, there is a need for more widespread training and education about these technologies among users with disabilities, caregivers, and the general public to ensure they are used effectively and safely.

USER DATA AND AI: UNDERSTANDING WHAT AI KNOWS ABOUT YOU

Something anyone who engages with AI wants—and deserves—to know is just how much AI knows about them. Understanding what AI knows about you and what it does with that information is instrumental in forming a relationship of trust with AI.

One of the biggest areas where user data is used by AI is in online interactions. AI systems play a big role in shaping your online experiences, subtly shaping those experiences based on many data points collected about you. Each time you browse a website, make an online purchase, or scroll through social media, AI systems gather data about your preferences, behaviors, and location. This data collection is not random or pointless; it is a targeted effort to understand your digital footprint, which in turn aids AI in creating a more personalized online environment for you. For instance, if you've ever wondered how a social media platform seems to know exactly what kind of products to advertise to you or how a streaming service recommends movies you end up loving, it's because of AI using the data you've provided without having to strenuously report that data yourself.

This process starts with collecting basic information, such as your device, IP address, and browsing history. More specific data points might include how long you spend on certain pages, the links you click, and even how you navigate a site. AI systems use this information to establish patterns and preferences that define your unique user profile. This profile is then used to adjust experiences across various platforms in a way that you will find more enjoyable. For example, AI can modify the layout of a news app to highlight sports stories if you frequently read articles about athletics, or it might prioritize showing you coffee-related products on e-commerce sites if you've searched for coffee machines recently.

Personalizing content and advertisements based on user data improves user experience immensely by making those experiences more engaging and efficient. You spend less time searching for what you need or discovering new content that aligns with your interests because AI places these things right on your feed. This not only makes your digital interactions more enjoyable but also increases the relevance of the advertisements you see, which can benefit both you and businesses aiming to reach their target audience more effectively.

It's natural to be concerned about the collection and use of personal data by AI systems. When it comes to these dilemmas, it's important for you to have control over what data is collected and how it is used. Many AI systems now incorporate mechanisms for user consent so that you are aware of and agree to data collection practices. These consent mechanisms are often part of user agreements or settings where you can specify which data types you are comfortable sharing. Additionally, many platforms provide options for you to view the data that has been collected and manage your preferences. For instance, you might decide to delete certain data or opt out of specific forms of data collection. Google Ads Analytics offers this feature. This level of control is imperative for maintaining your privacy and building trust between users and technology providers.

Protecting your data falls on the businesses collecting this data to protect the information of consumers, you included. Robust security measures are employed to protect this information and verify that it is being used responsibly. For example, encryption is a standard security technique used to protect data by making it unreadable to anyone without authorization to view it. This keeps your data safe from anyone you haven't consented to accessing your data. Secure servers and databases further shield your data from unauthorized access, and regular security audits help identify and rectify potential vulnerabilities. Moreover, as a user, you can enhance your data security by adopting strong, unique passwords for your online accounts, enabling two-factor authentication, and being cautious about the personal information you share online. These practices help mitigate the risk of data breaches and protect your personal information from being misused.

OVERCOMING TECH INTIMIDATION: AI FOR ALL AGES

As technology finds itself more and more involved with daily tasks once left to us to carry out on our own, the prospect of interacting with AI can seem intimidating to many, spanning from young students to elderly adults. The key to demystifying AI and making it accessible across all age groups is rooted in simplifying interactions with technology. By designing AI systems that utilize familiar interfaces and clear, straightforward instructions, the barrier to entry can be significantly lowered. For instance, a smart home device that uses simple, intuitive voice commands similar to everyday speech, or a health monitoring app with a straightforward, easy-to-navigate user interface are both going to represent technologies that anyone can use without barrier. These design choices can make a difference in helping everyone, regardless of their tech-savvy, feel comfortable and confident in using AI technologies.

Educational initiatives also have the potential to bridge the gap between AI and users. Across the world, various programs aim to educate the public about AI, offering resources that range from online courses for teenagers to workshops for seniors. These educational initiatives work to dispel myths and build understanding, showing that AI is not just a tool for the technically inclined but a part of everyday life that enhances our interactions with the world. For example, libraries and community centers often host sessions that teach attendees how to use AI in daily tasks, such as navigating smartphones or understanding social media algorithms. These sessions provide practical knowledge and foster a sense of community among learners so that the journey into the digital age is a shared and supportive experience.

The impact of these efforts is evident in numerous case studies where successful engagement with AI has significantly enhanced daily life across different age groups. For instance, consider a senior citizen who uses a voice-activated device to stay connected with family, manage medication schedules, and maintain independence in their home. Or a young student who uses AI-driven educational tools to personalize their learning and tackle subjects they find challenging. These examples highlight the practical benefits of AI and demonstrate how it can be adapted to meet diverse needs, enrich lives, and empower users, irrespective of their age or background.

Through thoughtful design, targeted educational programs, and strong community support, AI can be transformed from a source of intimidation into a valuable ally for users of all ages.

PRACTICAL AI: HANDS-ON APPLICATIONS AND PROJECTS

Understanding the "what" of AI's capabilities is just the beginning; this chapter will guide you through the "how" of harnessing AI's potential and integrating it into your everyday life. Here, we will take a look at practical applications of artificial intelligence that you can start using today. From crafting effective text-based prompts to leveraging AI to answer your questions, offer new content, or manage your personal finances, the possibilities are wide-ranging and accessible. We'll explore setting up AI home security solutions to keep your household safe and innovative ways to monitor and improve your health using AI technology. Additionally, we'll look into educational tools that make learning about AI engaging and interactive and guide you through the creative process of using AI to generate stunning artwork. All you need for this journey is a willingness to learn and a computer!

CHOOSING THE RIGHT TOOL

For beginners, choosing the right tool can make a significant difference in breaking into direct AI usage. A good starting tool offers versatility in the types of content it can generate and has robust support and tutorial resources that can guide you as you learn to interact more effectively with AI. Platforms like OpenAI's ChatGPT (Generative Pre-trained Transformer) offer user-friendly interfaces and extensive documentation to help you get started. These platforms are designed to be approachable, requiring no coding experience, which allows you to focus purely on crafting your prompts.

Below are just some of the AI tools available today. These AI tools have been designed to be user-friendly and can significantly enhance productivity, health, learning, and everyday convenience.

The following is a list of some of the most accessible AI options that you can start exploring as you seek to understand AI and what it does. Don't worry if you think this list will become outdated quickly. You can always ask AI to give you a current list of AI tools as well. For example, you might try prompting ChatGPT by asking, "What are some of the AI tools available for an average person who wants to use AI in their everyday lives?"

Productivity and Personal Assistance

- **ChatGPT:** An AI language model developed by OpenAI that can generate human-like text, answer questions, assist with writing tasks, provide conversational responses, and more.

- **Microsoft Copilot:** An AI-powered assistant integrated into Microsoft Office 365 applications, such as Word, Excel, and PowerPoint, it helps users draft documents, create presentations, analyze data, generate insights, and automate repetitive tasks.
- **Google Assistant, Apple Siri, Amazon Alexa:** These virtual assistants help set reminders, send messages, control smart home devices, and provide weather updates.
- **Notion AI:** This AI-powered productivity tool helps with note-taking, project management, and task organization.
- **Grammarly:** This AI-powered writing assistant helps with checking grammar, style suggestions, and plagiarism detection.

Health and Fitness

- **Fitbit, Apple Health, Google Fit:** These health-monitoring apps use AI to track physical activities, monitor heart rates, and provide personalized fitness recommendations.
- **MyFitnessPal:** An AI-based nutrition and diet app that tracks food intake, suggests meal plans, and helps manage caloric intake.

Finance Management

- **Mint, YNAB (You Need A Budget):** AI-driven personal finance tools that help manage budgets, track expenses, and provide financial insights.

- **Acorns:** An investment app that uses AI to round up your purchases to the nearest dollar and invest the spare change.
- **Betterment:** An automated investing platform that uses AI algorithms to provide personalized financial advice, optimize investment portfolios, and manage user funds
- **Wealthfront:** A robo-advisor that utilizes AI to offer personalized financial planning, automated investment management, and tax optimization strategies.

Home Automation

- **Smart Home Devices (Nest, Ring, Philips Hue):** These AI-integrated devices control home security systems, lighting, and climate for convenience and energy efficiency.

Education and Learning

- **Duolingo:** An AI-powered language learning app that adapts lessons based on user progress and learning style.
- **Khan Academy:** An educational platform that uses AI to provide personalized learning experiences in various subjects.
- **SoloLearn, Code.org, Scratch:** These programs provide user-friendly platforms where you can learn the fundamentals of coding in a fun and interactive way.

Creative Tools

- **DALL-E 2:** This AI tool by OpenAI generates images from text descriptions, which is helpful for artists and designers.
- **Canva:** A graphic design platform with AI features that assist in creating visually appealing designs and templates.
- **DeepArt:** DeepArt offers a user-friendly interface where you can transform your photos into artworks in the styles of famous painters like Van Gogh or Picasso.
- **AIVA:** For music composition, tools like AIVA (Artificial Intelligence Virtual Artist) allow you to create original music pieces.

Communication and Collaboration

- **Zoom, Microsoft Teams:** Video conferencing tools with AI features like background noise suppression, virtual backgrounds, and real-time translation.
- **Slack:** A collaboration tool with AI-driven features that help manage communications, prioritize messages, and integrate with other productivity apps.

Travel and Navigation

- **Google Maps, Waze:** These AI-powered navigation apps provide real-time traffic updates, route suggestions, and local business recommendations.

Shopping and E-commerce

- **Amazon, Alexa, Google Shopping:** These AI-driven shopping assistants help with product searches, price comparisons, and personalized shopping recommendations.

GETTING STARTED WITH TEXT-BASED PROMPTS

Text-based prompts are your way of communicating with a generative AI tool, telling it what kind of information or output you're seeking. Think of it as giving instructions to a highly efficient, utterly non-judgmental digital assistant. Whether you want a summary of the latest scientific research, a poem for your anniversary, or a concise report on stock market trends, it all starts with how you ask. Generative AI works its magic by understanding your prompt and creating text that can be impressively insightful, precise, and sometimes even clever, depending on what you've told it.

Designing Text-Based Prompts

Crafting effective prompts is an art form in itself. It requires a combination of clarity, specificity, and creativity. To start, always be clear about what you want. If you need a comprehensive list of the best Italian restaurants in your city, specify that. The more specific you are, the more personalized the AI's response will be. You can also ask the AI to adopt specific personas or writing styles, adding a layer of creativity to your interactions. For example, you might want the previous example to be written in the style of a food critic with a humorous tone.

Examples of Prompt Techniques

There are countless ways to prompt AI to work for you. Here are just a few examples:

- **Ask AI to "act as" a person on your behalf.** You can prompt this as, "Act as a financial advisor and suggest a budgeting plan to help me save for a down payment on a house."
- **Define the task specifically and clearly.** You can prompt, "Provide a brief overview of the most popular dog breeds in the United States?"
- **Provide examples**. You might command, "Write a short story about a young man who is shipwrecked, similar to *Robinson Crusoe.*"
- **Provide dos and don'ts.** For this, you could say, "Create a travel guide for a weekend trip to Paris. Do highlight popular tourist attractions and local cuisine. Don't include information about hotels or accommodation."
- **Set the tone and style.** You could prompt, "Give me a 200-word summary of the latest trends in winter fashion for senior women with a humous tone."

Illustration of a Prompt to ChatGPT and Resulting Response:

Sample Prompt	Sample ChatGPT Response
Act as a personal trainer for a 60-year-old man who has not worked out in years. Recommend 1 daily exercise to help him start a healthy lifestyle. Include an exercise that does not require equipment. Exclude walking.	As your personal trainer, I recommend starting with a simple yet effective daily exercise: **Bodyweight Squats.** **Bodyweight Squats:** **Why:** Squats are a great full-body exercise that strengthens your legs, core, and lower back. They also help improve balance and mobility, which is crucial as we age. **How to Perform:** 1. **Start Position:** Stand with your feet shoulder-width apart, toes pointing slightly outward. 2. **Engage Core:** Tighten your core muscles to stabilize your body. 3. **Lowering Down:** Slowly bend your knees and hips, lowering your body as if you are sitting back into a chair. Keep your back straight and your chest up. 4. **Depth:** Go down until your thighs are parallel to the ground or as low as you can comfortably go. 5. **Rising Up:** Push through your heels to return to the starting position, straightening your legs while maintaining good posture. **Repetitions:** Start with 10-12 squats, aiming for 2-3 sets. As you get stronger, you can gradually increase the number of repetitions or sets. **Tips:** • Focus on proper form rather than speed. • If balance is an issue, you can use a chair for support by holding onto the backrest lightly. • Remember to breathe out as you stand up and breathe in as you lower down. Starting with bodyweight squats can help you build a strong foundation and prepare your body for more challenging exercises as you progress.

When You Need Help Crafting a Prompt

You can even ask AI for assistance to create a prompt or clarify what additional information is needed, which is one of the most incredible displays of how AI is, in fact, intelligent. This is particularly useful when you are unsure how to frame a request to get the most relevant and accurate information from AI.

Illustration of a Prompt to ChatGPT Asking for Help Crafting a Prompt:

Sample Prompt	Sample ChatGPT Response

Can you help me write a prompt to get detailed information about renewable energy sources? I want to know about the different types, their benefits, and current technological advancements. Could you provide some examples and tips on how to structure my prompt request effectively?"	Certainly! When crafting a prompt to gather detailed information about renewable energy sources, you'll want to ensure that your request is clear, specific, and covers all the key areas you're interested in. Here's how you can structure your prompt:
	
	Prompt Structure:
	
	1. **Start with a Clear Request:**
	  o Begin by specifying what you want to know, such as "Provide detailed information about renewable energy sources."
	
	2. **Mention the Key Aspects:**
	  o Highlight the specific areas you're interested in, like types, benefits, and technological advancements.
	
	3. **Ask for Examples:**
	  o Request specific examples to better understand the application and impact of each renewable energy source.

4. Encourage Depth:
  o Ask for a thorough explanation to ensure you get in-depth information rather than just a surface-level overview.

Sample Prompt:

"Please provide a detailed overview of renewable energy sources, including the different types, their benefits, and current technological advancements. I would like to know about the most common types of renewable energy, such as solar, wind, hydropower, geothermal, and biomass. Additionally, explain the environmental and economic benefits of each type. Finally, include information on recent technological advancements that have improved the efficiency or accessibility of these energy sources, and provide specific examples where possible."

Tips for an Effective Prompt:

- **Be Specific:** Clearly outline what information you're looking for. The more specific your request, the better the response.

- **Break Down the Request:** If you're asking for multiple pieces of information (e.g., types, benefits, advancements), make sure to list them clearly.

- **Request Examples:** Asking for examples helps to clarify complex concepts and shows practical applications.

- **Encourage Depth**: Use phrases like "detailed overview" or "thorough explanation" to ensure the response goes beyond the basics.

Using these guidelines, you should receive a comprehensive and well-organized response that covers all aspects of renewable energy sources.

Iterate, Correct Mistakes, and Give Feedback

The interaction with AI continues after the first response. Often, you'll find that tweaking your prompt can significantly change the output. This iterative process helps refine the AI's understanding of your preferences and improves the accuracy and relevance of the information provided. If the list of restaurants includes too many upscale places and you prefer casual dining, adjust your prompt to reflect that preference. Each adjustment teaches the AI about your tastes, subtly enhancing its ability to serve you better.

This hands-on approach makes your use of AI more effective, personal, and satisfying. As you continue to interact with it, you'll learn not just about the extent and limits of artificial intelligence but also about your preferences and the clarity of your communication. These are valuable skills in a digital age where AI's role in our lives continues to grow.

Reflective Exercise: Crafting Your First AI Prompt

Take a moment to think about a daily task you find time-consuming or a question you've been curious about. Using the framework provided above:

- Write down a clear, specific prompt you could use to engage an AI in this task.
- Consider what style or tone you would like the AI to adopt in its response.
- Consider any additional information or constraints you might need to ensure a useful response.

- Finally, open up a generative AI tool like ChatGPT and experiment with prompting based on your above work.

This exercise will help you start your journey using text-based AI prompts effectively, making your interactions with AI functional and enjoyable.

SETTING UP AI FOR YOUR PERSONAL FINANCES

Managing personal finances can sometimes feel like navigating a maze without a map. However, the advent of AI in financial management has brought about tools that promise to simplify this journey and personalize it in previously unimaginable ways. From budget trackers that learn from your spending habits to investment advisors that tailor their advice based on your financial goals and risk tolerance, AI can transform how you manage your money.

Let's begin by exploring various AI tools and apps designed to assist in personal finance management. Budget trackers like Mint or YNAB (You Need A Budget), as mentioned earlier, use AI to categorize your spending automatically and provide insights into where your money goes each month. These tools can help you set spending limits and alert you when you're about to exceed them, which makes it easier to stick to your budget. On the investment side, robo-advisors such as Betterment and Wealthfront use algorithms to manage your investments and rebalance your portfolio automatically to align with your financial goals and market conditions. These tools make expert-level advice accessible to anyone with a smartphone and an internet connection.

Setting up an AI-powered budgeting tool is your first step toward understanding your financial health. Begin by choosing a platform that syncs easily with your bank accounts and credit cards. This integration allows the tool to pull in your transaction data automatically, saving you the effort of manual entry and ensuring that your financial overview is always up-to-date. Once your accounts are linked, take some time to explore the app's features. Set up budgets for different spending categories—like groceries, entertainment, and utilities—and check how the app tracks your expenses against these budgets over time. Many apps also offer personalized insights based on your spending patterns, suggesting areas where you can cut back or highlighting trends in your financial behavior. Take a look at these different features and see what they offer you in terms of aiding in money management.

Integrating AI into your financial planning involves more than just tracking expenses and investments, though. AI can also help with predictive forecasting of expenses—such as guiding you to anticipate and prepare for future financial needs. For example, suppose you're saving for a major purchase, like a home or a car. AI tools can analyze your saving rate and market conditions to estimate how quickly you'll reach your goal and even provide feedback about how you can meet your goal faster. These tools can also alert you to potential financial risks, such as cash flow shortages, allowing you to adjust your spending or saving behavior before problems arise. For investments, AI can suggest opportunities based on economic trends and your personal risk profile so that you can make informed decisions that align with your long-term financial goals.

When using AI for personal finance, it's necessary to think about privacy and security, just like with any technology that deals with sensitive information. Make sure that any app or tool you use has strong security features in place, such as encrypting your data and using secure ways to verify your identity. Be cautious of apps that ask for unnecessary access permissions, as these could potentially expose your financial information to outside companies. Always take the time to read the privacy policy so you understand how your data will be used and stored.

AI HOME SECURITY SOLUTIONS

The practical applications of AI also extend to home security. Imagine sitting in the comfort of your home. With a few taps on your smartphone, you can check who's at your front door, monitor your backyard, or even get alerts if any unusual activity is detected. This marks an incredible change in how you're able to elevate your home's security using AI-driven systems that integrate effortlessly into your daily life. AI in home security has evolved beyond traditional alarm systems to incorporate advanced features like facial recognition and real-time activity alerts, adding a new proactive and responsive security layer to the mix.

Using AI for home security comes along with significant benefits. For instance, cameras with AI integrations can analyze live video footage to distinguish between ordinary activities and potential threats. If an unknown person is loitering by your front door or odd movement is detected late into the night, the system can alert you instantly so that you can take action. Beyond that, AI capabilities can extend to recognizing family members, frequent visitors, and even pets, reducing false alarms—a common issue with traditional motion detectors. This intelligent recognition makes it more likely that you're only alerted when there's a genuine need.

Setting up AI security cameras is often a first step in using AI for home security. It might sound like a task requiring technical expertise, but it's pretty straightforward. You should start by choosing AI-enabled security cameras that offer features suited to your specific needs, such as night vision, weather resistance, and Wi-Fi connectivity, all depending on what you most desire and need for your home. Installation is simple; it typically involves mounting the cameras at strategic points around your property so that they cover all entry points and areas like driveways and gardens. Most modern AI cameras are designed for easy setup, often requiring you to mount the camera and connect it to your home Wi-Fi network through a smartphone app. This app becomes your command center, allowing you to view live feeds, receive alerts, and even communicate through built-in speakers on the cameras. In short, with a couple of taps and a good place to mount your cameras, you can have your very own AI-led security system in no time.

From there, you might also want to consider integrating AI with home automation systems, which can bolster your home security by linking cameras with other smart devices. For example, let's say that your AI security camera detects movement outside your home at night. It can use that input to automatically trigger outdoor lights or send a signal to close garage doors, which adds an extra layer of deterrence against potential intruders. These integrations can be customized to fit your lifestyle and security preferences, providing a security system that not only alerts you to potential dangers but also actively works to prevent them.

While setting up such a comprehensive AI-driven security system in your home, it's vital to consider the legal and privacy implications in doing so, both for yourself and those around you. Surveillance cameras, especially those with recording capabilities, can lead to privacy concerns among neighbors and visitors. Because of this, verifying that your security setup complies with local laws regarding video surveillance and data protection is essential. Always position your cameras in a way that they monitor your property only and avoid areas where privacy expectations are high, such as neighbor's windows or public pathways. Also, the data collected by AI cameras should be securely stored and protected from unauthorized access.

As you think about enhancing your home security with AI, remember that these technologies are designed to add convenience and peace of mind to your life. With the proper setup, responsible usage, and adherence to legal standards, AI-driven security systems can offer safety and a sense of security that allows you to enjoy your home with greater assurance and less worry.

USING AI TO IMPROVE YOUR HEALTH MONITORING

In an era where our smartphones are almost as familiar with our habits as we are, the leap to using AI-powered health-tracking apps is a small but significant step toward proactive personal health management. Earlier, we discussed how AI is breaking into the field of health monitoring. We're going to expand that discussion now because these apps do far more than merely track your steps or count calories; they analyze patterns in your physical activity, sleep, and dietary habits to offer insights that can lead to healthier lifestyle choices. For example, by monitoring your sleep patterns, an AI app can suggest the best times to go to bed and wake up, optimizing your sleep cycle for better mental and physical health. Similarly, in tracking your food intake, these apps can identify nutritional gaps in your diet and offer suggestions that are customized to your specific health needs and goals.

Setting up a Personal Health Dashboard

In order to reap these benefits, you have to set up your own personal health dashboard. Setting up a personal health dashboard integrates data from various AI health apps to create a comprehensive view of your health that's informative and easily accessible. There are dozens of apps available for this, each offering unique features that can suit your needs. Begin by picking out health apps that cover different wellness aspects, such as physical activity, nutrition, sleep, and mindfulness—depending on what your goals are. Many smartphones already offer health monitoring systems that can serve as a hub for integrating data from various apps, thus reducing the amount of setup effort on your part. If you're hoping for a more detailed view, choose a dashboard app that lets you customize which data points you want to monitor and how they are displayed. This customization makes it so that you have all the relevant information at your fingertips, readily available whenever you unlock your phone. It also empowers you to set personal health goals and track your progress.

AI and Early Detection

Perhaps one of the most incredible aspects of AI in health monitoring is its capability to detect early signs of health. There are many ways that AI can do this. For example, by continuously analyzing data on your heart rate, activity levels, and other vital signs, AI can identify patterns that may indicate emerging health issues before they become serious. A sudden decrease in physical activity combined with increased resting heart rate, for instance, could alert you to potential health problems that require medical attention to prevent more serious conditions from developing. Early detection is instrumental in managing health issues more effectively, often leading to better outcomes and lower medical costs.

While AI-driven health insights can be incredibly valuable, balancing them with professional medical advice is non-negotiable. AI tools are designed to supplement, not replace, the expertise of medical professionals. Always consult with a healthcare provider to interpret AI health data correctly and make informed decisions about your health. For example, if your AI health app suggests potential signs of a sleep disorder, discuss these findings with your doctor to verify the diagnosis and explore treatment options.

EDUCATIONAL TOOLS: LEARNING AI THROUGH APPS

Thanks to AI, accessing educational resources has never been more simple—and that includes learning about AI directly as well. AI educational apps offer tools that impart knowledge while adapting to their users' individual learning styles and paces. These apps are designed to make learning about AI and coding accessible and truly engaging for everyone, regardless of age or educational background. Using AI-powered educational apps, you can start from the basics of AI concepts and gradually advance to more complex topics, all at your own pace and comfort.

For those beginning their journey into the world of AI, apps like SoloLearn, Code.org, and Scratch offer user-friendly platforms where you can master the fundamentals of coding in a fun and interactive way. These apps offer bite-sized lessons that are easy to digest and interactive quizzes that help reinforce what you've learned.

Interactive learning through AI-powered educational tools brings to the table several benefits that traditional learning environments often lack. These apps use adaptive learning technologies to structure educational content according to your learning speed and the specific areas where you need more focus. For example, if you struggle with a particular programming concept, the app can offer additional exercises to help you master it before moving on to the next topic. This personalized learning approach means that you are not just passively receiving information—rather, you're actively engaging with the material for better retention and efficacy.

Many of these apps boost their engagement because they incorporate gaming elements into their learning modules, which can transform your education into an enjoyable and motivating experience. Challenges and coding games make the application of AI concepts fun and rewarding. For instance, you might be tasked with using AI to solve puzzles or build simple models, activities that provide practical experience and theoretical knowledge. These engaging projects solidify your understanding of AI and spark your creativity, encouraging you to think outside the box and apply what you've learned in innovative ways. As a result, your ability to use AI in practical settings is only strengthened.

A GUIDE TO CREATING ART WITH AI

For many people, the world of AI-generated art is one of the most compelling ways that we can directly work with AI. The fusion of technology and creativity has opened up new doors in the arts, with AI now playing a pivotal role in the creative processes of many artists, musicians, and designers. Today, AI-driven tools are doing more than just assisting artists; they are also becoming collaborators in the creative process by offering up new ways to innovate and express ideas.

Platforms such as DeepArt, DALL-E 2, Canva, and AIVA, to name a few, grant artists the tools needed to create everything from intricate paintings and sculptures to moving music compositions. These platforms use algorithms that analyze existing artworks to generate new pieces that actually engage and have meaning for humans like us. They offer users a range of controls to influence the final output so that each creation is as unique as its human collaborator.

How to Create AI Art

To begin creating AI-generated art, choose a platform that aligns with your artistic goals:

- **Visual Art with DeepArt:** DeepArt offers a user-friendly interface where you can transform your photos into artworks in the styles of famous painters like Van Gogh or Picasso. Start by uploading a base image—the subject of your artwork—and then select a style from the platform's extensive library or upload one of your own. The AI will then process the image, applying the chosen style and rendering a new piece that merges your original photo with the artistic flair of your selected style.
- **Innovative Creations with DALL-E 2:** DALL-E 2, developed by OpenAI, allows users to generate highly detailed images from textual descriptions. You can start

by describing the image you want to create and DALL-E 2 will generate a series of images based on your description. This tool is particularly powerful for conceptual art and visualization, enabling artists to create entirely new scenes, objects, or characters that do not yet exist.

- **Designs with Canva:** Canva is an AI-powered design platform that simplifies the creation of graphic designs, from social media posts to professional presentations. Its AI features include design suggestions, automatic layout adjustments, and a vast library of templates and elements that you can customize. By using Canva, artists and designers can quickly bring their creative visions to life, even if they have limited design experience.

- **Music Composition with AIVA:** For music composition, tools like AIVA allow you to create original music pieces. Here, you would start by selecting your piece's base genre or mood. The platform provides various templates based on different musical styles and structures. You can input specific parameters such as tempo, key, and instruments, or let the AI make these decisions based on the mood you've chosen. The AI then processes these inputs to compose a unique piece of music, which you can refine by adjusting certain elements or re-running the AI with different settings.

By leveraging these AI-driven tools, artists and creators can explore new dimensions of creativity to produce innovative works that blend human ingenuity with the power of artificial intelligence.

Understanding AI's Role in Creativity

AI's role in the creative process is multifaceted, supporting human creativity by automating routine parts of the creative process and providing fresh perspectives. For example, in graphic design, AI tools can automatically generate layouts and color schemes so that designers can focus their efforts more on content and overall aesthetics. Similarly, in writing, AI can suggest plot developments or dialogue options, helping writers overcome creative blocks. This partnership between AI and human creativity is mutually beneficial; AI provides the tools and suggestions, while human creators bring context, emotion, and personal expression, which are crucial for the art to resonate on a human level.

As AI tools become available, you don't have to take a backseat to their advancements. Jumping in and mastering prompting, integrating AI apps into your life, and understanding the ethical implications of AI in different areas of life can empower you to make informed decisions about AI and use AI tools to improve your life.

MAKE A DIFFERENCE WITH YOUR REVIEW

Unlock the Power of Sharing

Helping others feels pretty amazing, doesn't it? And guess what? It can make a huge difference in someone's life—someone you might never meet, but who needs a little guidance just like you once did.

My goal with The Complete Beginner's Guide to AI is simple: to make understanding AI easy and accessible for everyone. I want to break down the walls that make AI seem tricky or too complicated or even scary. But to do that, I would love to reach as many people as possible. That's where you come in.

Think about it—most people decide to read a book based on its cover and, yep, you guessed it, its reviews. So, I'm asking you to help out a fellow beginner in AI who might feel a bit lost right now.

Please take just a minute to leave a review for this book.

It won't cost you anything, and it takes less than 60 seconds, but it could make a world of difference. Your review might be the one that helps...

... one more student grasp a new concept.
... one more curious mind feel confident exploring AI.
... one more future tech leader take their first step.

To get that warm, fuzzy feeling of knowing you've helped someone, all you have to do is leave a review. It's quick and easy—just scan the QR code below:

If helping others feels as good to you as it does to me, welcome to the club!

Thank you so much for your support. Now, let's get back to exploring the amazing world of AI together!

Your biggest fan, Gloria Lembo

ETHICAL AI: NAVIGATING THE MORAL LANDSCAPE

Throughout the last five chapters, we've worked with key innovations in AI to understand their potential and impact on our everyday lives. In doing so, we also touched on the ethical implications surrounding AI. Now, however, it's time to really examine the ethical world of AI. This chapter delves into these pressing issues, exploring the relationship between technological progress and ethical responsibility. Taking the time to really appreciate and comprehend the moral landscape of AI means being able to ensure your own privacy and data protection despite the ever-changing world of AI advancements.

PRIVACY AND SURVEILLANCE: THE BALANCING ACT

Imagine you're walking through a city where cameras on every street corner feed into an AI system, continuously analyzing the flow of individuals. These cameras aren't just passive observers but part of a complex network designed to enhance public safety, optimize traffic, and even identify wanted criminals. Integrating

AI into our public spaces isn't a futuristic concept—it's today's reality in many parts of the world. However, with such technological advancements come significant ethical questions, particularly concerning privacy and surveillance. How do we balance the benefits of AI-enhanced safety with the fundamental right to personal privacy?

Defining Personal Privacy

In the digital age, personal privacy is more than the simple right to be left alone. It also includes the ability to control information about oneself and decide how much information others can access. AI technologies, which often rely on large amounts of data harvested from users to function optimally, challenge these boundaries. Every interaction with digital devices—social media, online shopping, or even public Wi-Fi—generates data that AI systems can collect and analyze. The ethical use of this data is necessary, as it involves sensitive information that, if mishandled, can lead to harmful privacy breaches. Understanding personal privacy in this context requires us to think about what information is collected and how it is used, who has access to it, and how we can retain control over our data.

Surveillance by AI

AI in surveillance has become increasingly common in both governmental and private sectors. Cities around the world are employing AI-based technologies for various purposes; this includes monitoring traffic and public spaces and optimizing security measures against crime. While the intentions behind these uses are often well-meaning—geared toward protecting the public and optimizing urban functionality—they also lead to privacy concerns.

For instance, facial recognition technology can help identify missing persons or suspects. Still, it can also lead to a scenario where everyone's movements are tracked, blurring the line between public interest and personal privacy invasion. As these technologies become more ingrained in our world, the people implementing them consistently ask themselves how balances may be struck between personal privacy and public safety, especially in the realm of surveillance.

Balancing Benefits and Risks

The trade-offs between enhanced security and privacy erosion are a central concern being discussed in the ethics of AI surveillance. On one hand, AI can significantly improve public safety by quickly identifying potential threats and optimizing emergency responses. For example, AI systems in smart cities can analyze data from various sensors and cameras to predict and manage everything from traffic jams to natural disasters, potentially saving lives and resources.

On the other hand, these systems can collect an immense amount of personal information, much of which is gathered without explicit consent or even the awareness of the individuals it concerns. Balancing these benefits and risks requires technological solutions that protect individuals' privacy without hindering the public benefits AI can bring, something that is constantly in the works as such technologies come to life.

Reflective Exercise: Evaluating Personal Data Privacy

Take a moment to reflect on your interactions with technology today:

- Consider the devices and services you use that may collect your data. Do you know what data they collect and how they use it?
- Assess your current privacy settings on these platforms. Are there adjustments you could make to protect your privacy better?
- Think about how you might balance the benefits of AI technologies with your personal privacy preferences. Where would you draw the line?

Thinking about these questions can help you better understand AI's implications for your privacy and encourage a more informed and proactive approach to managing your data in the digital age.

BIAS IN AI: RECOGNITION AND MITIGATION STRATEGIES

In an ideal world, the tools and systems we use would treat everyone fairly, without prejudice or bias. However, as AI becomes increasingly integrated into different aspects of our lives—from deciding who gets a job interview to determining eligibility for loans—it's clear that these systems can, and do, inherit and even amplify human biases. The sources of bias in AI are diverse, stemming from the data it's trained on, the way algorithms are structured, and even the objectives set by human designers. For example, a hiring tool trained on historical employment data might use data that reflects past discriminatory practices.

Because of this, the AI might learn to replicate these biases, favoring specific demographics over others.

The impact of such biases can be far-reaching, especially in critical areas like criminal justice, hiring practices, and financial services. In criminal justice, AI tools are used to assess the risk of reoffending. However, if these tools are trained on skewed data that reflects racial biases, they could disproportionately flag minority groups as high-risk. In hiring, AI that screens resumes can overlook qualified candidates from underrepresented backgrounds if trained on data that mirrors existing workplace imbalances. In the financial sector, algorithms that determine creditworthiness could perpetuate historical inequalities, denying loans to individuals based on biased data points linked to race, gender, or zip code.

To avoid these biases, it's vital to recognize and understand where they come from. One effective strategy that can be used in developing these tools is diversifying the datasets used to train AI systems. By ensuring these datasets represent all sections of society, we can reduce the risk of one-sided, biased learning outcomes. For example, many tech companies are now actively seeking more diverse facial datasets to train their recognition algorithms so that accuracy can be improved across different demographics. Another useful approach is implementing regular bias audits. AI systems would then be periodically reviewed to identify and correct biases that may have seeped into their operations, and then those biases can be untrained.

Embedding ethical considerations into the very design of AI systems is another strategy that can reduce bias and lead to fairness in how these systems are implemented. This involves setting clear guidelines on the ethical use of AI, which should be aligned with broader human values and rights. It also means involving diverse stakeholders in developing and deploying AI technologies. By bringing diverse perspectives, such as the perspectives of ethicists and sociologists, to the communities most likely to be impacted by AI, we can ensure a more holistic approach to ethical AI development. This inclusive process helps spot potential biases and create a broader understanding of the social implications of AI technologies.

AI AND EMPLOYMENT: ADDRESSING JOB DISPLACEMENT CONCERNS

When you hear about artificial intelligence in the workplace, it's easy to envision robots taking over jobs, leaving humans in the dust as a result. The reality, however, is more nuanced and less dire than AI replacing each of us in our current jobs. Think about all of the tasks at your job that you wish you didn't have to do and the ones you'd love to spend more time on because of how fulfilling they are. This is something that AI can create for the future of labor. AI and automation are transforming the nature of work across various sectors, but this transformation is not about job displacement. Instead, the focus is, and should be, on job evolution and creation. Understanding this is necessary for navigating the future workforce landscape effectively.

AI's impact on jobs looks different depending on which industry you examine. In manufacturing, automation has increased production efficiency and shifted the types of jobs available. Repetitive and hazardous tasks are increasingly delegated to machines, which perform them with greater precision and without fatigue. However, this doesn't necessarily mean a reduction in the workforce. Instead, the role of the human worker evolves to involve more complex problem-solving and oversight tasks, such as overseeing AI systems and managing responses to unexpected situations. Similarly, in sectors like retail, AI has transformed jobs through inventory management systems and checkout automation—freeing retail employees up to focus on more human-centric aspects of the job. It has also created new roles in IT support, system maintenance, and customer service management, where human skills are irreplaceable.

The shift to an economy influenced by AI highlights how important it is for people to learn new skills and adapt. The world is always changing, and AI is another change that we have to accommodate—just like the invention of the internet was something to adapt to. Education and training programs are useful in getting the workforce ready for these changes. Successful efforts often involve partnerships between governments, schools, and businesses. For example, IBM's P-TECH model guides students from high school through community college to careers, focusing on skills needed in today's tech-driven world (IBM Makes Education & Hiring 2020). Similarly, Google's Career Certificates prepare people for jobs in growing fields like data analytics and user experience design, even if they don't have a traditional college degree. These programs teach technical skills and highlight critical thinking and problem-solving, which are vital as AI becomes more common in the workplace.

Again, the inclusion of AI in the workforce isn't about limiting opportunity. The rise of AI in fact brings significant economic opportunities by incentivizing innovation and boosting productivity. AI tools can analyze massive amounts of data to uncover insights and trends that humans might miss, leading to smarter decision-making and advancements in product and service development. For example, AI algorithms can streamline supply chains, predict when machines need maintenance, and personalize customer interactions, all of which enhance efficiency and cut costs. AI's role here isn't to replace humans but to enhance our abilities, freeing us to focus on strategic tasks requiring human creativity and insight. Ultimately, this leads to more fulfilling labor because our efforts are more meaningful than what completing repetitive tasks directly provides.

However, addressing the challenges AI poses to jobs requires social safety nets. Policies like improved unemployment benefits have the potential to provide security to workers transitioning between jobs or facing job loss due to automation. For example, during periods of major industry shifts, temporary income support can give workers stability to retrain or find new job opportunities. Continuous learning programs, backed by employers and government initiatives, also help ensure that the workforce remains adaptable and thrives in a rapidly changing job market. Advocating for positive considerations for workers' rights is one of many ways that you can help shape the future of AI.

SELF-DRIVING VEHICLES: ETHICS OF DECISION-MAKING IN MACHINES

Imagine cruising down a highway in an autonomous vehicle (AV), where the steering wheel moves under the guidance of sophisticated algorithms, sensors, and cameras. As you relax in the passenger seat, the vehicle suddenly faces an unavoidable dilemma: swerve to avoid a pedestrian who has unexpectedly stepped onto the road or maintain course, risking harm to the pedestrian but protecting you and other passengers. This scenario, known as the "trolley problem," is a classic ethical dilemma that has gained new relevance in the age of autonomous vehicles. Such dilemmas highlight the complex decision-making processes that must be programmed into AVs, raising questions about machine morality and the ethics of outsourcing life-or-death decisions to algorithms.

The challenge of programming ethics into AI systems, particularly autonomous vehicles, revolves around the variability of human ethics and cultural differences. Each person has a unique answer to the trolley problem and what is considered to be the "right" choice. Ethical decision-making in humans involves a complex equation of cultural background, personal values, and situational context, all of which can vary widely from one person to the next. When translating these decision-making processes into algorithms, developers have to decide which ethical principles to prioritize. For instance, should an AV always minimize harm, or should it prioritize the safety of its passengers at all costs?

Liability and Accountability

As autonomous vehicles navigate our streets, they also create a world of considerations regarding liability and accountability. Determining responsibility can be challenging when an AV is involved in an accident. Traditional vehicular accidents typically attribute liability to one or more drivers based on negligence or violation of traffic laws. However, with AVs, the "driver" is an algorithm, raising the question of who is responsible when something goes wrong. Is it the manufacturer of the vehicle, the developer of the AI software, the operator of the service, or the owner of the car?

This issue is further complicated because AI systems can learn and adapt over time. A decision-making process that leads to an accident may result from machine learning algorithms evolving in unforeseen ways. This characteristic of AI means that traditional concepts of liability, which are based on predictability and intent, aren't able to be upheld as easily. Legal frameworks worldwide work with these questions in an attempt to create regulations protecting public safety while promoting innovation in autonomous vehicle technologies.

Public Trust and Acceptance

The widespread acceptance of autonomous vehicles relies on public trust, which is deeply influenced by how well ethical and moral challenges are addressed. Trust is built on transparency, consistency, and the assurance of safety. If the public perceives AVs as unsafe or ethically unpredictable, their adoption will likely be slow and characterized by resistance. In contrast, clear communication about how AVs make decisions, robust safety records, and transparent responses to accidents can help build public confidence.

Public trust is also shaped by how autonomous vehicles are integrated into society. For example, if AVs significantly reduce accidents and traffic congestion, demonstrate reliable and ethical decision-making in emergencies, and are accessible to a wide range of users, they are more likely to be embraced by the public. On the other hand, if introduced in a way that disrupts current transportation systems, leads to job losses in driving professions without adequate provisions for retraining and support, or is only accessible to certain people, public trust toward AVs could be undermined.

AI IN LAW ENFORCEMENT: POTENTIAL AND PITFALLS

AI and ethical considerations are slowly finding their way into the world of law enforcement. Particularly, AI is heightening efficiency, but it is also posing ethical considerations both for existing law enforcement efforts and for AI-operated enforcement systems that may be more prevalent in the future. AI tools such as predictive policing, facial recognition, and data analysis are being employed more and more often by police forces around the world.

Predictive policing algorithms take a look at data from previous police activity to forecast criminal activity, directing police resources to areas where crimes are more likely to occur. This proactive approach works to prevent crimes before they happen, which can potentially reduce crime rates and make police work more efficient. However, relying on historical data can also perpetuate existing biases, targeting specific communities disproportionately if the data reflects past prejudices.

Facial recognition technology, another AI tool, is used in various scenarios, from identifying suspects in crowds to finding missing persons. While the technology can significantly enhance the capability of law enforcement agencies to solve crimes, it also raises profound privacy concerns. The ability of governments to track individuals without their consent has been criticized as a step towards a surveillance state, where one's privacy is constantly compromised. The use of AI in data analysis, which can sift through massive datasets to find patterns and correlations, also presents a dual-edged sword. On the one hand, it can uncover valuable insights that might go unnoticed by human analysts; on the other hand, it can lead to conclusions that may be invasive or incorrect if the data is not handled or interpreted appropriately.

Balancing the benefits of enhanced public safety with protecting individual rights and civil liberties is a delicate task. Law enforcement agencies must navigate the fine line between using technology to protect citizens effectively and ensuring that the same technology does not infringe upon the rights those citizens are entitled to. This balance requires careful consideration of how AI tools are implemented and strong oversight mechanisms to prevent misuse. For instance, regular audits of AI systems and the data used can help identify and mitigate biases. Moreover, involving community representatives in the oversight process can help ensure that the use of AI in policing aligns with community values and needs, fostering a collaborative approach to public safety.

THE ETHICS OF AI IN WARFARE: A CLOSER LOOK

The deployment of artificial intelligence in military contexts is a rapidly evolving prospect that combines cutting-edge technology with some of the oldest human endeavors—defense and warfare. Autonomous drones patrolling the skies and AI systems making strategic defense decisions are no longer just concepts; they are current realities that present remarkable capabilities and significant ethical dilemmas alike. As AI continues to permeate various aspects of military operations, its role ranges from operational support to active engagement in combat scenarios.

AI-driven systems in the military offer strategic advantages that are hard to overstate. Autonomous drones, for example, can perform surveillance missions without putting human lives at risk, gathering important data that can be used to make informed decisions quickly. These drones can operate in environments that are too hazardous for human troops, thus providing constant surveillance without fatigue and with fewer logistical requirements. At the same time, AI systems can process large chunks of data from different intelligence sources much faster than human teams—identifying patterns and threats that might not be immediately observed by human analysts. This capability can result in a more responsive and adaptive military strategy that increases the effectiveness and precision of military operations.

Naturally, the integration of AI into military technology is not without its controversies, particularly concerning Lethal Autonomous Weapons Systems (LAWS). These systems, which can select and engage targets without human intervention, represent a significant shift in the conduct of warfare (Etzioni and Etzioni 2017). The debate over LAWS is intense and multifaceted, involving ethical, legal, and security dimensions. Ethically, the main concern is the delegation of life-and-death decisions to machines. Can an AI system adequately understand the nuances of a combat situation well enough to make decisions about human lives?

The ongoing international debate over LAWS also highlights broader security concerns. There is an inherent fear that deploying autonomous weapons could lead to an arms race in military AI technologies, potentially leading to global instability. Countries may feel compelled to develop or acquire autonomous weapons to keep up with their adversaries, which could then escalate military tensions and make international diplomacy more complicated as a result. Furthermore, the risk of these systems being hacked or malfunctioning could lead to unintended engagements with catastrophic consequences.

Given these significant issues, regulating AI in warfare is a critical area of international policy. Efforts at both national and international levels are focused on creating frameworks that can effectively govern the use of AI in military applications. Key treaties and agreements, such as those under the United Nations Convention on Certain Conventional Weapons (CCW) are being examined and expanded to include provisions specific to autonomous weapons (Convention on Certain Conventional Weapons n.d.). These discussions aim to set limits on the use of such technology so that AI advancements in the military respect international law and the principles of ethical warfare.

SETTING GLOBAL STANDARDS: WHO REGULATES AI?

As strong as technology's influence is in the world of you and me, this influence isn't so strong in other areas of the world. Some demographics and regions have access to modern information and communication technology, but others do not. AI has the potential to either bridge or widen this gap. For example, AI-driven educational platforms can offer personalized learning experiences to students in remote areas, potentially leveling the academic playing field. However, if access to these technologies remains concentrated in wealthier, urban areas, the gap may widen and leave rural and lower-income regions further behind. This disparity demonstrates the need for concerted efforts to make AI technologies accessible to all, not just the economically or geographically privileged.

AI for Global Good

AI's capacity to serve the greater good is immense, particularly in addressing global challenges like hunger, health, and education. Initiatives like AI for Good, led by the United Nations, harness AI's power to accelerate the achievement of the United Nations Sustainable Development Goals (AI for Good Summit 2024). Examples include using AI to analyze satellite images to enhance agricultural yields in underdeveloped countries or AI-driven platforms that can diagnose diseases in areas lacking sufficient medical professionals.

The Need for Global Standards

The need for global standards in AI is evident as its applications cross borders and impact societies worldwide. Without a unified regulatory framework, deploying AI technologies can result in a patchwork of standards, leading to inconsistencies that could undermine consumer protection, privacy, and ethical guidelines. Establishing global AI standards is the best way to manage these international ethical, legal, and social implications. Such standards need to address AI's technical aspects, such as safety and reliability, and their broader impacts on privacy, security, and human rights.

Key international players like the European Union (EU), the United Nations (UN), and the Organization for Economic Co-operation and Development (OECD) are primarily responsible for setting these global AI guidelines and standards. The EU's approach to AI regulation focuses on transparency, accountability, and ensuring that AI systems are subject to human oversight (Pouget and Zuhdi 2024). Similarly, the OECD principles on AI promote innovative and trustworthy AI that respects human rights and democratic values (OECD n.d.). Through its various agencies, the UN also aids in addressing the ethical implications of AI, ensuring that it benefits all of humanity, not just a select few (Azoulay 2018).

However, achieving international consensus on AI regulations isn't as easy as it might seem at a glance. Differing cultural and political perspectives can influence what is considered ethical or acceptable regarding AI deployment. For instance, the European emphasis on privacy and data protection is not universally prioritized to the same extent in other regions. Also, the rapid pace of AI development means that technology often evolves faster than regulatory environments, necessitating a flexible and adaptive approach to governance.

Despite these challenges, effective AI regulation and standards have emerged around the world. Singapore's Model AI Governance Framework is one example of this. It focuses on providing detailed and clear guidance for the ethical deployment of AI (Singapore's Approach to AI Governance n.d.). It has been recognized internationally for its comprehensiveness and applicability across different sectors. Similarly, the Dubai AI Principles offer a framework for ethical AI implementation that aligns with the city's specific needs and growth strategies (Principles of Artificial Intelligence n.d.).

As AI becomes more and more overt in the world around us, being able to identify ethical concerns and understand how they affect you is one of the most important ways to remain in control and use AI as a companion rather than a replacement or authority. Staying up-to-date on how these AI moral concerns unfold benefits everyone, including you.

THE FUTURE OF AI: EMERGING TRENDS AND FUTURE INNOVATIONS

Any form of technology is bound to have developments that lead to future innovations, and AI is no different. While the landscape of AI currently appears one way, the future that it can unlock has the potential to be vastly different in an overwhelmingly positive way. As you continue to explore AI, understanding what the future might look like as it grows and becomes more intelligent is an empowering way to drive improvements in your life and the lives of those around you.

QUANTUM COMPUTING AND AI: UNLOCKING NEW POTENTIALS

Quantum computing serves as an incredible shift in how we handle data. Unlike traditional computers that use bits to represent information (either 1 or 0), quantum computers utilize qubits, which can exist in states of both 1 and 0 simultaneously due to a phenomenon called superposition. This unique capability allows quantum computers to explore countless possibilities simultaneously, making them exceptionally powerful for tasks beyond the scope of classical computers.

Quantum computing has the potential to significantly enhance AI systems when integrated alongside them. For example, AI models that require processing massive datasets to learn and make decisions could benefit from drastically reduced training times when quantum computing is incorporated. This is because quantum computers excel at efficiently analyzing and processing large datasets compared to classical computers. Furthermore, quantum algorithms can optimize machine learning models by improving their efficiency and enabling quicker and more precise decision-making.

Potential Applications

The practical applications of quantum AI are diverse. In drug discovery, quantum AI could change how we simulate molecular interactions, therefore accelerating the discovery of new drugs and supporting our understanding of diseases at a molecular level. This could then lead to faster development of more effective treatments. Similarly, in logistics and manufacturing, quantum AI could solve complex optimization problems, such as efficiently managing supply chains or improving manufacturing processes to minimize waste and maximize output.

Current Research and Developments

Globally, there is significant research underway to harness quantum computing for AI applications. Universities, tech companies, and startups are heavily investing in quantum research, with notable breakthroughs already achieved. For example, Google's quantum computer, Sycamore, demonstrated "quantum supremacy" by performing a computation in 200 seconds that would take a supercomputer approximately 10,000 years—and that's not an exaggeration either (Swayne 2024). While not directly related to AI, this achievement models quantum computing's potential to tackle currently unsolvable problems.

Barriers to Adoption

Despite its promise, there are certain barriers to integrating quantum computing into AI. Technologically, developing stable and reliable quantum computers remains difficult due to the sensitivity of qubits to their environment, such as temperature changes or vibrations, which can introduce errors. Financially, the costs of building and maintaining quantum computing infrastructure are high, often reaching billions of dollars. This limits access to large organizations.

There is a significant educational barrier to adopting this technology, including a shortage of quantum scientists and engineers. Quantum computing also requires a deep understanding of quantum mechanics, which is not yet widely integrated into standard computer science education. Efforts from governments and educational institutions are necessary if we hope to overcome these barriers, including funding research, incentivizing partnerships, and incorporating quantum computing into educational curricula to train the next generation of quantum experts.

AI AND BLOCKCHAIN: A NEW LAYER OF POSSIBILITIES

Blockchain is a type of technology that serves as a secure and decentralized digital ledger. It consists of a chain of blocks, each containing a list of records or transactions. These blocks are linked together using cryptography, forming a continuous and permanent chain. One of the key features of blockchain is its decentralized nature, meaning that the ledger is not stored in a central location but is distributed across a network of computers referred to as nodes. This ensures transparency and security, as transactions recorded on the blockchain are visible to all participants and cannot be altered retroactively without altering all subsequent blocks.

Blockchain technology is best known for its initial application in cryptocurrencies like Bitcoin, but its potential uses can be applied to various industries, including finance, supply chain management, healthcare, and more, where secure and transparent record-keeping is helpful and ethical.

Blockchain as a Security Layer for AI

Blockchain technology can greatly improve the security and transparency of AI systems. Each decision made by an AI system can be recorded on a blockchain to create a permanent and unchangeable record of the decision-making process. This is helpful because it creates an audit trail that can be reviewed by external auditors or regulatory bodies, making certain that the AI operates as intended without manipulation. For example, in financial services where AI automates trading decisions, blockchain can provide a clear and tamper-proof trail of all actions taken by the AI software, which is essential for solidifying compliance and trust. The immutability of blockchain means that once a record is made, it cannot be altered, thus preventing fraud and raising the efficiency of security for AI applications (Shamsan Saleh 2024).

Decentralized AI Applications

Blockchain's decentralization has introduced a new approach to AI applications. In traditional AI models, the power and control over AI systems are often centralized within a few large corporations or entities with the resources to develop and maintain such systems. However, blockchain allows for a decentralized model where AI algorithms run on a distributed network maintained by multiple stakeholders. As a result, the centralization of power is decreased and the accessibility of AI is increased. For example, a decentralized AI model for predictive healthcare could be run by a network of hospitals, research institutions, and healthcare providers, each contributing data and resources to improve the model's accuracy and reliability. This collaboration can then lead to more equitable AI applications where the benefits of AI are shared more broadly across society.

Impact on Data Privacy and Ownership

Integrating AI with blockchain could also revolutionize data privacy and ownership. In many AI applications, users often relinquish control over their data to AI companies, which use the data to train and improve AI models. Blockchain can change this dynamic by allowing users to maintain control of their data on a decentralized network. Users can share their data with AI systems through smart contracts that specify how it can be used and for what purpose. This approach empowers them and opens up new business models where users can be compensated for their data, creating a more balanced and fair data economy. For instance, in a blockchain-based AI system for personalized marketing, users could opt to share their shopping preferences and receive targeted advertisements while receiving tokens or digital currency as compensation for sharing their data.

Challenges and Limitations

Integrating blockchain with AI is challenging, even if it has incredible potential. One of the primary challenges of this integration is scalability. Blockchain networks, especially fully decentralized ones, can suffer from slow transaction speeds and high processing costs, which can be a hurdle for AI applications that require real-time processing and large volumes of data. Additionally, integrating AI and blockchain requires significant technical expertise in both domains, which can be a barrier for organizations looking to adopt this technology.

The regulatory landscape for blockchain and AI is still evolving as well, which poses even more challenges. As these technologies create new ways of managing data and making decisions, they also raise new legal and ethical considerations that regulators have to address. Navigating this regulatory environment can be complex and uncertain for companies pioneering these integrated solutions.

THE RISE OF AUTONOMOUS ROBOTS: BEYOND FACTORY FLOORS

AI's advancement also means that we are looking at the potential for autonomous robots in the near future. The expansion of autonomous robots into service industries and public sectors is a testament to technological advancements and a shift toward more integrated, service-oriented robotics applications in everyday life.

In healthcare, robots are being deployed for various tasks, from routine sanitation to more complex roles like assisting in surgeries or managing medication dispensation. This isn't limited to physical tasks; AI-driven robots are also used to monitor patient health stats and predict medical needs based on AI analysis.

Similarly, in public service roles like policing or firefighting, robots equipped with AI are used for tasks that are too dangerous for humans. They can enter burning buildings to locate people or assess the structural integrity of a compromised building, providing real-time data to human teams to make informed decisions.

Human-Robot Interaction and Collaboration

The interaction between humans and robots is evolving, marked by a significant improvement in the collaborative capabilities of robots. Modern robotic systems are designed to understand and predict human actions to some extent, leading to smoother cooperation. For example, in surgical settings, robots can pass the necessary surgical tools to the human surgeon at the right time, having "learned" the surgery sequence. Similarly, in elderly care, robots can be used for physical assistance and as social companions that can engage with older adults, thus providing interactions that can help reduce feelings of loneliness.

These advancements are all thanks to the intricate AI algorithms that enable robots to learn from their environments and adapt to new tasks quickly. This adaptability is vital in environments like hospitals or disaster sites, where the situation can change unpredictably. Machine learning continually enhances the safety and efficiency of these collaborative efforts, as robots learn from each interaction and become more adept at predicting and responding to the needs of their human counterparts.

Ethical and Employment Considerations

As you may have guessed the widespread adoption of autonomous robots brings its own set of ethical and employment concerns. Among the most voiced concerns is job displacement. As robots become capable of performing more complex tasks, there is an understandable worry about the impact on employment in traditional roles. However, while some jobs may be reduced or transformed, new opportunities are created in areas like robot maintenance, programming, and system management. Also, the focus is increasingly on human-robot collaboration rather than replacement, where robots assist humans to achieve higher productivity and safety.

Ethically, deploying robots, especially in sensitive sectors like healthcare and public safety, can bring up inquiries regarding privacy, decision-making in critical situations, and the potential for errors. For instance, should a robot be allowed to make necessary health decisions for a patient? What happens if a robot makes a mistake in a high-stakes situation like firefighting? Addressing these concerns is possible through clear guidelines and robust frameworks for the responsible use of robotics in such fields.

Case Studies of Successful Implementations

Real-world examples in Singapore and Japan of successful robot integration showcase advanced applications across different sectors:

Singapore

- **Healthcare:** Singapore employs robots in healthcare settings, especially for tasks like patient care, medication delivery, and assistance in surgeries. These robots help alleviate manpower shortages and improve efficiency in healthcare services (Ang 2024).
- **Public Services:** In public spaces, robots are used for cleaning and security purposes. Automated cleaning robots help maintain cleanliness in public areas, while security robots patrol and monitor to enhance safety (Babin 2024).
- **Logistics and Delivery:** Robots are utilized for logistics and delivery services. They navigate autonomously in warehouses to transport goods efficiently, contributing to streamlined operations in logistics hubs (Collaborative Urban Delivery Optimisation n.d.).
- **Education:** In educational institutions, robots are used to enhance learning experiences. They may serve as educational aids, teaching tools, or even as companions for children with special needs, fostering interactive and engaging learning environments (Tech and Education 2023).

Japan

- **Manufacturing:** Japan is a leader in industrial robotics, employing robots extensively in manufacturing processes. These robots perform tasks ranging from assembly and welding to quality control, contributing to Japan's advanced manufacturing capabilities (Barron 2023).
- **Elderly Care:** With an aging population, Japan has developed robots designed to assist elderly individuals in daily activities. These robots can provide companionship, monitor health metrics, and offer physical assistance, addressing caregiver shortages and promoting independent living (Mori 2023).
- **Hospitality:** Robots are utilized in Japan's hospitality industry, particularly in hotels and restaurants. They may serve as receptionists, concierges, or waitstaff, enhancing customer service and efficiency in service delivery (Djokaj 2023).
- **Entertainment and Culture:** Japan embraces robots in entertainment and cultural contexts. From robot-themed cafes to robot exhibitions and performances, robots contribute to Japan's vibrant cultural landscape and attract tourists interested in futuristic experiences (Inoue 2024).

In these implementations, the key to success has been the careful integration of robots into human teams so that they supplement rather than replace human efforts. Continuous feedback loops, where human workers can provide insights into the robot's performance, have been helpful in refining these robotic systems.

AUGMENTED REALITY MEETS AI: NEXT-LEVEL INTERACTIONS

Augmented reality has swiftly moved from gaming and entertainment into more practical, everyday applications, greatly altering how we interact with the digital world. This transformation is primarily fueled by advancements in AI, which have dramatically enhanced AR technologies as we know them. AI is key in improving image recognition so that AR systems can accurately understand and interact with the natural world in immediate ways. Imagine pointing your smartphone at a restaurant and instantly seeing reviews, menu highlights, and even the day's special offers superimposed on your screen. This is a very real possibility because of AI algorithms that process and augment real-world images in milliseconds, granting a seamless and informative experience.

Spatial mapping is another area where AI elevates AR, which allows digital objects to interact realistically with physical environments. This technology helps your device to understand and map the environment around you so that when you place a digital object, like a piece of furniture in a room, it appears naturally as part of the space, respecting boundaries and sizes relative to other objects and walls. This feature is common on sites for furniture stores, for example, making it easier for you to visualize interior design choices and make the perfect purchase without ever having to leave the comfort of your own home.

Interactive elements that respond intelligently to user inputs are also altering AR experiences. These elements, powered by AI, can change based on user interactions. For example, in educational AR applications, a student learning about human anatomy might point their device at a human body model and tap on various organs to see detailed information and realistic simulations of how they function. The AI recognizes these inputs and provides relevant, interactive content that improves learning, making it a dynamic and engaging process.

Applications in Education and Training

Integrating AI with AR completely changes the game of educational methodologies by providing immersive, interactive learning experiences that adapt to individual learning styles and paces. In medical training, for example, future developments in AR overlays have the potential to provide students with 3D visualizations of anatomical structures, allowing them to explore complex details from different angles by simply moving their tablet or wearing AR glasses. This hands-on approach would help students grasp complex concepts more quickly and retain information longer.

Professional training environments also stand to benefit from AI-enhanced AR by simulating real-world scenarios where trainees can practice without the risks associated with actual operations. Consider a mechanic who can practice assembling an engine through AR before touching the real thing. The AI system assesses their actions, provides real-time feedback, and adjusts the difficulty of the task based on their performance. This personalized feedback loop not only accelerates the learning curve but also ensures a high standard of training, which is particularly valuable in fields where precision and accuracy are paramount.

Retail and Marketing Innovations

In retail, AI-driven AR can influence how consumers interact with brands and products. Retailers that use AR apps create a chance for customers to try on clothes virtually or see how a piece of furniture would look in their home before making a purchase. These apps use AI to analyze the shape and dimensions of the space or the person and then render the products realistically within those parameters. This elevates the shopping experience and reduces the likelihood of returns, as customers have a better sense of how the product fits into their lives.

Marketing campaigns also benefit from AR as they increasingly incorporate it to produce engaging and memorable experiences that drive consumer interaction and brand loyalty. For example, a cosmetic company could use an AR filter on a social media platform that allows users to try different makeup looks. Powered by AI, the filter would adjust the makeup colors and styles based on the user's features and preferences to facilitate a personalized experience that encourages users to engage with the brand more deeply.

Future Potential and Challenges

The future of AI in AR holds incredible promise, with potential applications expanding into virtually every sector, from real estate, where clients could take virtual tours of properties, to tourism, where travelers could use AR to access real-time information about landmarks. However, realizing this potential fully requires overcoming several challenges. Technologically, improving the accuracy and responsiveness of AR systems is key to creating digital augmentations that are seamless and realistic. This requires even more sophistication from AI algorithms in order to process vast amounts of data in real time without draining device batteries.

Societally, there are significant considerations around privacy and data security, as AR systems often collect detailed information about users' environments and behaviors. Developing strong, fool-proof privacy protections and promoting transparency about how data is used are essential strategies for maintaining user trust and creating an atmosphere where these technologies are happily welcomed. Additionally, as AR becomes more prevalent, there is a need to verify that these technologies are accessible to all to prevent the digital gap from widening.

PREDICTING THE NEXT DECADE: WHERE AI IS HEADED

Looking ahead to the next decade, artificial intelligence could change how we live every day faster than we anticipate. Expected AI advancements won't just upgrade algorithms, hardware, and apps; they'll also reshape our societies and economies. These changes will bring new chances for growth but also bring tough challenges to overcome.

Trends and Predictions in AI Development

The next decade in AI development may lead to unprecedented advancements in algorithms and hardware, driving more sophisticated and efficient AI applications. Current trends suggest a significant leap in machine learning techniques, with algorithms becoming more adept at processing unstructured data such as images, videos, and natural language. This will likely lead to AI systems that are not only faster but also more intuitive in understanding human contexts and nuances.

The evolution of AI hardware, driven by the need for more processing power, is expected to see innovations such as neuromorphic chips—hardware that mimics the neural structures of the human brain even more accurately than neural networks are able to in their own contexts. These chips promise to dramatically reduce energy consumption and increase the speed of AI computations, making AI systems more accessible and integrated into smaller, everyday devices.

Simultaneously, the application of AI is set to broaden, with significant impacts expected in sectors like healthcare, where AI could lead to personalized medicine tailored to individual genetic profiles. In environmental management, AI might predict and manage natural disasters with greater accuracy, potentially saving lives and reducing economic losses. These advancements will hinge on technological breakthroughs and collaborative efforts that bridge different fields of expertise, from data science to ethical governance.

Impact on Society and Economy

Integrating advanced AI systems into various sectors will likely lead to profound societal and economic impacts as well. Economically, AI could drive growth through increased productivity and the creation of new markets and industries. For example, the automation of routine tasks could free up human labor for more complex and creative tasks, which would then lead to higher job satisfaction and innovative outputs. But this shift might also cause problems, like displacing workers from traditional roles, unless considerations are made with these concerns in mind. Without strong policies and training programs, this could widen income gaps and worsen existing economic disparities.

In society as a whole, AI has the potential to improve our lives by offering personalized services and more convenience. Yet, it could also raise privacy concerns because advanced AI might need to gather and use large amounts of personal information without our direct consent. Balancing these benefits and risks will need open discussions across all parts of society. This will help make sure AI grows in ways that match everyone's interests and ethical rules.

Preparing for the Future

Preparing for the changes brought by AI is crucial. For governments, this means investing in education systems that can adapt to the demands of an AI-driven economy, emphasizing skills such as critical thinking, creativity, and digital literacy. Policies must also be flexible to quickly adapt to AI advancements, emphasizing innovation while protecting people's rights. For industries, the focus should be on building strong infrastructure to support AI technologies. This includes physical things like data centers and networks, as well as digital infrastructure such as cybersecurity and data management. These measures ensure that AI systems are secure and reliable.

As the future of AI becomes increasingly certain, it's easy to lapse into fear about what uncertainties will unfold as a result. While we can never be perfectly sure of what will happen with AI, keeping yourself informed about advancements as they unfold will improve your confidence and comfort with these technological advancements. To help you out with this, our final chapter will concentrate on how you can stay informed.

STAYING INFORMED AND ETHICAL IN THE AI WORLD

AI is always changing. Who knows—we might wake up tomorrow and find out that some advancement has completely reoriented AI as a whole! While we can't always know what's next to come, as the people who AI will affect, we owe it to ourselves to stay up to date on what's happening in the world of AI. Doing so means keeping up with the news, participating in community discussions, and otherwise knowing how to navigate and understand advancements as they unfold.

KEEPING UP WITH AI NEWS WITHOUT OVERWHELM

When the news is constantly full of novel ideas and innovations, or scary doomsday predictions, it's easy to become overwhelmed by everything there is to read, watch, and take note of. This doesn't have to be the case, however. Keeping up with the news becomes simple when you know which sources to trust and how to filter for the most relevant information.

Curating Reliable Sources

Getting accurate information is crucial, especially in a complex and rapidly developing field like artificial intelligence. To keep up with these changes, start by finding reliable sources that provide up-to-date AI news with journalistic integrity and expertise. Look into respected tech news sites, AI research journals, and publications known for in-depth analysis and expert insights. Websites such as Wired, TechCrunch, and MIT Technology Review's AI section are good places to begin. They feature articles by knowledgeable writers who keep up with the latest in AI, ensuring you get current and trustworthy information.

Additionally, consider subscribing to newsletters from leading AI research institutions like the Allen Institute for AI or industry leaders like Google's AI Blog. These newsletters provide direct insights from AI experts, covering new research, industry trends, and ethical debates. They offer a deeper look into specific AI topics you're interested in learning more about.

Using Aggregators and Filters

To manage the flow of information effectively without overwhelming yourself, you can consider using news aggregators and filters. Tools like Feedly or Google News allow you to create customized feeds based on specific topics such as artificial intelligence, machine learning, or AI ethics. You can further refine these feeds by setting filters for your favorite news sources, preferred authors, or the most mentioned keywords. This personalizes your news intake and saves time by consolidating articles from various sources into a single, manageable stream.

Furthermore, these aggregators often use AI to learn from your reading habits, gradually honing the selection of articles presented to you based on what you read, share, and save. This makes the tool more effective at filtering out noise and increasing relevance so that the information you receive is streamlined to your ongoing educational journey in AI.

Critical Reading Skills

Developing critical reading skills is necessary for understanding AI news, especially considering how some news outlets will make unfounded claims to provoke fear or uncertainty. Focus on reputable sources that specialize in technology rather than general news outlets. Look for articles that cite sources, present data, and include quotes from experts—these indicate well-researched content. Also, be cautious of sensational headlines that might exaggerate the impact of new AI developments. Always read the full article to grasp the context and any limitations in the studies or technologies discussed. This makes sure that you're well-informed and able to discuss AI confidently and with a balanced perspective.

PARTICIPATING IN AI COMMUNITY DISCUSSIONS

Navigating the world of artificial intelligence can often feel like you're hearing a foreign language, especially when you're new to the field. But just like learning any new language, immersing yourself in AI through community interactions can drastically elevate your understanding and fluency. Engaging with online forums and communities dedicated to AI simplifies complex topics and enriches your learning experience with diverse perspectives and expert insights.

Finding the Right Forums

There are several excellent online AI community forums where you can engage in discussions, ask questions, and stay updated on AI trends and developments. Here are a few popular ones that you can explore:

- **r/Artificial on Reddit:** A subreddit dedicated to discussions on artificial intelligence, machine learning, and robotics. It's a vibrant community with a mix of professionals, enthusiasts, and researchers sharing news, and articles, and engaging in discussions.
- **Artificial Intelligence on Stack Exchange:** Part of the Stack Exchange network, this community-driven Q&A site allows users to ask and answer questions related to AI. It's structured around specific questions and answers, making it easy to find information on various AI topics.
- **AI Community on LinkedIn:** LinkedIn hosts numerous AI-related groups and communities where professionals, researchers, and enthusiasts discuss AI trends, job opportunities, research papers, and industry news.

These forums provide valuable opportunities to connect with the AI community, stay informed about the latest developments, and participate in discussions on various AI topics.

AI INVESTMENT: WHAT YOU NEED TO KNOW

Artificial intelligence is a rapidly growing sector, which logically attracts investors and companies keen on tapping into its vast potential. The AI market is a complex environment featuring various individuals and organizations, including established tech giants, innovative startups, and specialized AI firms. Companies like Google, Amazon, and IBM continue to invest heavily in AI, developing technologies that range from advanced machine learning algorithms to practical applications such as voice recognition and autonomous driving. Meanwhile, emerging startups are pushing to further AI innovation by focusing on niche areas like AI for healthcare diagnostics or AI-driven cybersecurity solutions.

Here are some notable AI companies that investors often consider, which you can explore to broaden your understanding of how the AI investment world is currently operating:

- NVIDIA (NVDA): It is known for its GPUs (Graphics Processing Units) that are widely used in AI and machine learning applications, including deep learning training and inference.
- Alphabet (GOOGL): Google's parent company, Alphabet is heavily invested in AI research and development across its products and services, including Google AI, Waymo (autonomous vehicles), and DeepMind (AI research).
- Amazon (AMZN): Everyone's favorite online retailer utilizes AI for its cloud computing services (AWS - Amazon Web Services), recommendation engines, logistics optimization, and voice assistant Alexa.
- Microsoft (MSFT): Microsoft is home to the Azure AI platform, cognitive services, and investments in AI-powered solutions across productivity tools, cloud computing, and gaming (e.g., Minecraft AI).
- IBM (IBM): With an offering of Watson AI services for businesses, IBM focuses on AI applications in healthcare, finance, and cybersecurity, among others.

- Tesla (TSLA): Known for its advancements in autonomous driving technology, Tesla leverages AI and machine learning for its vehicles' self-driving capabilities.
- Salesforce (CRM): It uses AI for its customer relationship management (CRM) platform, including predictive analytics and AI-powered customer service solutions.
- Intel (INTC): This well-known technology giant provides AI hardware solutions, including processors and accelerators optimized for AI workloads.
- C3.ai (AI): It focuses on enterprise AI software solutions, including predictive analytics, IoT (Internet of Things), and AI applications across industries.

Investing in AI—something that you might be personally interested in—involves navigating potential risks and rewards, both of which are pronounced in this high-stake technology landscape. One of the significant risks is technological obsolescence. AI technology evolves at an exceptionally fast pace, and today's cutting-edge innovations can quickly become outdated as new advancements emerge. This rapid cycle can affect the longevity and profitability of AI investments. Market volatility is another risk factor, with AI companies often operating at the forefront of technology. Here, they face high levels of uncertainty and competition, which can lead to significant fluctuations in their market value.

On the flip side, the rewards of investing in AI can be intense. This technology is set to play a major role in future economies and has the potential to generate significant returns as it transforms major industries. The key is to approach AI investments with a strategic perspective, focusing on long-term impacts and the sustainable growth of AI technologies.

Lastly, the concept of sustainable and ethical investing in AI is gaining traction. Investors are beginning to increasingly recognize the importance of considering the broader societal impacts of their investment choices. Sustainable AI investing, for example, involves supporting companies that use AI to address pressing global challenges such as climate change, healthcare, and education. On the other hand, ethical investing focuses on promoting AI technologies that are developed and used according to ethical guidelines and best practices to promote fairness, transparency, and respect for user privacy.

Before investing in any company, it's important to conduct thorough research and consider the company's financial health, growth prospects, and how AI fits into its overall strategy. Consulting with a financial advisor can also help you access personalized guidance based on your investment goals and risk tolerance.

TEACHING KIDS ABOUT AI: A RESPONSIBLE APPROACH

Introducing children to AI concepts prepares them for future careers and shapes informed, ethical, and adaptable future citizens. If you're an educator or parent, understanding how to introduce children to AI can be particularly helpful for you and those around you. AI is already part of our daily lives—from the algorithms that filter the videos they watch to the smart devices that respond to their voices. Teaching kids about AI from an early age can help them understand its impact on their lives.

To start, make sure that you tailor the complexity of AI concepts to different developmental stages using age-appropriate language and examples. For younger children, this might involve explaining AI through stories or characters they are familiar with, such as robots that learn to understand and respond to their needs. Simple concepts like recognizing patterns, foundational to understanding AI, can be taught through fun activities like sorting games or matching patterns in nature or artwork.

As children grow older, these foundational ideas can be expanded into more complex discussions about how different apps or devices use AI to function. Middle schoolers, for instance, can handle more technical explanations, like how AI uses information from various sources to make decisions or recommendations. Hands-on projects, such as programming a simple robot or using online AI tools to create art or music, can make these concepts tangible and engaging. These activities teach practical skills and allow kids to see the results of AI processes firsthand, bridging the gap between theoretical knowledge and real-world application.

Instilling ethical thinking about AI from a young age is equally important. For example, discussions about fairness in AI decisions can be framed around familiar situations, such as how a game decides who gets to go first or how a music streaming service decides which songs to play next. This can lead to deeper discussions about the importance of fairness and transparency, not just in games or music but in more significant areas like job applications or loan approvals as they age. In addition, the privacy implications of digital assistants that respond to voice commands can be explored through questions like, "How do you feel about a device that can listen and respond to you? What should it do or not do with the information it hears?" These conversations can teach children to question how technology works and consider the ethical implications of its use in everyday life.

Preparing children for a future where AI will be ubiquitous also means helping them hone essential skills like critical thinking, problem-solving, and adaptability. Encouraging children to ask questions, think critically about the answers they receive, and consider alternative solutions to problems will prepare them to navigate a world where AI tools and automated decision-making are the norms. These skills will empower them to adapt to new technologies and challenges they will inevitably face as AI evolves and reshapes various aspects of society.

CONCLUSION

From the outset, our goal has been to unravel the mysteries of artificial intelligence for you. We've delved into AI's intricate concepts, witnessed its integration into everyday technology, learned some of the tools available to us, and navigated the ethical world shaping its impact on society.

Artificial intelligence is far more than just an incredible piece of technology. It's a guiding force sweeping through various sectors of modern society in ways that will change the world as we know it. From advancing healthcare with predictive diagnostics to reshaping financial markets through automated trading, AI's influence continues to expand, which serves to emphasize the importance of understanding it. Throughout each chapter, we've uncovered how AI is reshaping education, enhancing personal and professional efficiency, and posing ethical questions that demand thoughtful consideration.

The knowledge you've gained throughout this book equips you with the foundational understanding needed to engage with AI confidently. Whether you're interacting with AI-driven devices, implementing AI in your professional projects, or simply staying informed about the latest trends, you're now better prepared to harness AI's potential in ways that are both meaningful and responsible.

Final Thoughts

AI is a powerful force that, when used wisely, can unlock incredible potential. It is both an exciting opportunity and a significant responsibility. By understanding AI, applying it thoughtfully, and considering its ethical implications, you can be part of a future where AI enhances our lives in profound and positive ways.

Thank you for taking this journey into AI with me. The future is bright, and with the knowledge you've gained, you are now better equipped to navigate and shape the world of AI.

KEEPING THE AI JOURNEY ALIVE

Now that you've got all the tools and insights you need to dive into the world of AI, it's time to share what you've learned and guide others on the same exciting path.

By leaving your opinion of *The Complete Beginner's Guide to AI* on Amazon, you'll help other curious minds discover the same knowledge that helped you. Your review will light the way for fellow beginners, showing them that AI isn't so scary after all—it's something anyone can understand and enjoy.

Thank you for being part of this journey. AI is an ever-evolving field, and by sharing what you've learned, you're helping to keep the spirit of exploration and learning alive.

Scan the QR code below to leave your review on Amazon.

Let's keep the AI conversation going and inspire more people to take their first step into this incredible world. Your help means the world to me—and to all the future AI explorers out there.

Thank you!

Gloria Lembo

REFERENCES

"AI for Good Summit: Digital and Technological Divide Is No Longer Acceptable." 2024. UN News. May 30, 2024. https://news.un.org/en/story/2024/05/1150451.

"Ang, Adam. 2024. "Behind Singapore's Widespread AI Adoption in Public Health." Healthcare IT News. January 24, 2024. https://www.healthcareitnews.com/news/asia/behind-singapores-widespread-ai-adoption-public-health.

Anyoha, Rockwell. 2017. "The History of Artificial Intelligence." *Science in the News | Harvard Griffin GSAS* (blog) August 28, 2017. https://sitn.hms.harvard.edu/flash/2017/history-artificial-intelligence/.

Azoulay, Audrey. 2018. "Towards an Ethics of Artificial Intelligence." United Nations. December 2018. https://www.un.org/en/chronicle/article/towards-ethics-artificial-intelligence.

Babin, Nicolas. 2024. "AI and Government Services Optimization: The Singapore Smart Nation Initiative." LinkedIn. March 5, 2024. https://www.linkedin.com/pulse/ai-government-services-optimization-singapore-smart-nation-babin-ad7re/.

Banoula, Mayank. 2023. "What Is Perceptron: A Beginners Guide for Perceptron." Simplilearn. May 10, 2023. https://www.simplilearn.com/tutorials/deep-learning-tutorial/perceptron.

Barron, Michael. 2023. "Japanese AI Is Reshaping Industries and Economy." GlobalEdge (blog). September 27, 2023. https://globaledge.msu.edu/blog/post/57299/japanese-ai-is-reshaping-industries-and.

"Biggest Artificial Intelligence Stocks in the Market Today." 2024. *MMC Alumni (blog)*. January 24, 2024. https://mmcalumni.ca/blog/biggest-artificial-intelligence-stocks-in-the-market-today.

Buehler, T. Leigh. 2024. "Artificial Intelligence in Retail and Improving Efficiency." American Public University. March 4, 2024. https://www.apu.apus.edu/area-of-study/business-and-management/resources/artificial-intelligence-in-retail-and-improving-efficiency/.

Chen, James. 2019. "Algorithmic Trading Definition." Investopedia. 2019. https://www.investopedia.com/terms/a/algorithmictrading.asp.

Cherniak, Kateryna. 2024. "Chatbot Statistics: What Businesses Need to Know about Digital Assistants." *Master of Code Global* (blog). June 21, 2024. https://masterofcode.com/blog/chatbot-statistics.

Clifford, Alexander. 2024. "A Complete Guide on AI-Powered Personal Assistants with Examples." *Medium* (blog). February 1, 2024. https://medium.com/@ alexander_clifford/a-complete-guide-on-ai-powered-personal-assistants-with-examples-2f5cd894d566.

"Collaborative Urban Delivery Optimisation (CUDO)." n.d. AI Singapore. https:// aisingapore.org/aiproducts/cudo/.

Conrad, Ryan. 2024. "AI in Logistics: Driving Sustainability and Efficiency in Supply Chains." RTS Labs. March 1, 2024. https://rtslabs.com/ai-logistics-sustainabil ity-efficiency#:

DigitalOcean. 2023. "Understanding AI Fraud Detection and Prevention Strategies." Www.digitalocean.com. 2023. https://www.digitalocean.com/resources/arti cle/ai-fraud-detection.

Djokaj, Marija. 2023. "Henn-Na Hotel: Where AI Meets Hotel Industry." *Hochschule Luzern* (blog). May 31, 2023. https://blog.hslu.ch/majorobm/2023/05/31/ wadjokaj-2/.

Etzioni, Amitai, and Oren Etzioni. 2017. "Pros and Cons of Autonomous Weapons Systems." Army University Press. June 2017. https://www.armyupress. army.mil/Journals/Military-Review/English-Edition-Archives/May-June-2017/Pros-and-Cons-of-Autonomous-Weapons-Systems/

Fattepure, Sameer. 2023. "AI Ethics in Action: Real-World Examples and Best Practices." *Medium* (blog). July 27, 2023. https://medium.com/@Future-AI/ai-ethics-in-action-real-world-examples-and-best-practices-b57ba83c94ca.

Giles, Martin. 2018. "The GANfather: The Man Who's given Machines the Gift of Imagination." *MIT Technology Review* (blog). February 21, 2018. https://www. technologyreview.com/2018/02/21/145289/the-ganfather-the-man-whos-given-machines-the-gift-of-imagination/.

Google. n.d. "Supervised vs. Unsupervised Learning." Google Cloud. https://cloud. google.com/discover/supervised-vs-unsupervised-learning.

Great Learning Team. 2024. "Types of Neural Networks and Definition of Neural Network." *Great Learning* (blog). July 25, 2024. https://www.mygreatlearning. com/blog/types-of-neural-networks/.

"How AI Image Generators Work: An In-Depth Explanation" | artAIstry. https:// artaistry.com/blogs/ideas/how-ai-image-generators-work-an-in-depth-explanation

"IBM Makes Education & Hiring More Inclusive Worldwide with P-TECH Model Expanding across 28 Countries." 2020. IBM Newsroom. November 17, 2020. https://newsroom.ibm.com/2020-11-17-IBM-Makes-Education-Hiring-More-Inclusive-Worldwide-with-P-TECH-Model-Expanding-Across-28-Countries.

Inoue, Yukana. 2024. "Is AI a Friend or Foe of the Japanese Entertainment Industry?" The Japan Times. January 5, 2024. https://www.japantimes.co.jp/ business/2024/01/05/tech/ai-in-japanese-entertainment/.

Johnson, Arianna. 2023. "You're Already Using AI: Here's Where It's at in Everyday Life, from Facial Recognition to Navigation Apps." Forbes. April 14, 2023. https://www.forbes.com/sites/ariannajohnson/2023/04/14/youre-already-using-ai-heres-where-its-at-in-everyday-life-from-facial-recognition-to-navigation-apps/.

Karjian, Ron. 2023. "The History of Artificial Intelligence: Complete AI Timeline." TechTarget. August 16, 2023. https://www.techtarget.com/searchenterpriseai/tip/The-history-of-artificial-intelligence-Complete-AI-timeline.

Kawano, Jorge. 2024. "Leverage the Full Potential of AI to Predictive Maintenance." Vidya. April 10, 2024. https://vidyatec.com/blog/why-is-ai-so-crucial-for-predictive-maintenance/#:

Llego, Mark Anthony. 2023. "Promoting Societal and Environmental Impact Awareness within the AI-Driven Holistic Development Framework for Education." TeacherPH. March 22, 2023. https://www.teacherph.com/societal-environmental-impact-awareness-ai-driven-holistic-education-framework/.

Lutkevich, Ben. 2019. "What Are Self-Driving Cars and How Do They Work?" TechTarget. October 2019. https://www.techtarget.com/searchenterpriseai/definition/driverless-car

Marr, Bernard. 2023. "15 Amazing Real-World Applications of AI Everyone Should Know About." Forbes. May 10, 2023. https://www.forbes.com/sites/bernardmarr/2023/05/10/15-amazing-real-world-applications-of-ai-everyone-should-know-about/.

Max_zero. 2023. "The Pros, Cons and Costs of Autonomous Tractors. A Deep Look at Robotic Tractors." Agtecher: The Agri Tech Place. November 9, 2023. https://agtecher.com/autonomous-tractors-pros-cons/.

"Maximizing Engagement with AI Personalization: Strategies for the Modern Marketer." 2024. Kumo.ai. 2024. https://kumo.ai/resources/blog/ns-newsarticle-maximizing-engagement-with-ai-personalization-strategies-for-the-modern-marketer#:

"Mitigating Bias in Artificial Intelligence." n.d. Berkeley Haas. https://haas.berkeley.edu/equity/resources/playbooks/mitigating-bias-in-ai/.

Moluguri, Vinay Kumar. 2023. "Google's Teachable Machine AI: Step-By-Step Tutorial Included." Medium (blog). August 12, 2023. https://vinaykumarmoluguri.medium.com/googles-teachable-machine-ai-step-by-step-tutorial-included-6a7200199932.

Mori, Shotaro. 2023. "AI-Powered Robot Keeps Dementia Patients Company in Japan." Nikkei Asia. June 19, 2023. https://asia.nikkei.com/Business/Health-Care/AI-powered-robot-keeps-dementia-patients-company-in-Japan.

Mouajib, El Mahdi. 2024. "Navigating the Global AI Governance Landscape: From Voluntary Standards to Legally Binding Rules." Teneo. March 26, 2024. https://

www.teneo.com/insights/articles/navigating-the-global-ai-governance-land scape-from-voluntary-standards-to-legally-binding-rules/.

Mulaveesala, Manu. 2023. "A Non-Technical Introduction to AI: Part 1." Medium. *Medium* (blog). May 5, 2023. https://medium.com/@manutej/a-non-technical-introduction-to-ai-part-1-a53471fae2fe.

Needhi, Jeyadev. 2024. "The Role of AI in Wildlife Conservation: A Case Study of Anti-Poaching Efforts in Africa." Medium. Medium. July 10, 2024. https://medium.com/@jeyadev_needhi/the-role-of-ai-in-wildlife-conservation-a-case-study-of-anti-poaching-efforts-in-africa-d5b5c4e8e53f.

OECD. n.d. "OECD AI Principles Overview." https://oecd.ai/en/ai-principles.

Ognjanovski, Gavril. 2019. "Everything You Need to Know about Neural Networks and Backpropagation—Machine Learning Made Easy...." *Medium* (blog). January 14, 2019. https://towardsdatascience.com/everything-you-need-to-know-about-neural-networks-and-backpropagation-machine-learning-made-easy-e5285bc2be3a.

Pazzanese, Christina. 2020. "Great Promise but Potential for Peril." The Harvard Gazette. October 26, 2020. https://news.harvard.edu/gazette/story/2020/10/ethical-concerns-mount-as-ai-takes-bigger-decision-making-role/.

Pizzuto, Celia. 2024. "Revolutionizing Mobility with Advanced AI-Powered Exoskeletons." AI for Good. June 24, 2024. https://aiforgood.itu.int/revolutionizing-mobility-with-advanced-ai-powered-exoskeletons/.

Pouget, Hadrien, and Rahj Zuhdi. 2024. "AI and Product Safety Standards under the EU AI Act." Carnegie Endowment for International Peace. March 5, 2024. https://carnegieendowment.org/research/2024/03/ai-and-product-safety-standards-under-the-eu-ai-act?lang=en.

"Principles of Artificial Intelligence." n.d. Digital Dubai. https://www.digitaldubai.ae/initiatives/ai-principles.

ProjectPro. 2024. "10 NLP Techniques Every Data Scientist Should Know." April 11, 2024. https://www.projectpro.io/article/10-nlp-techniques-every-data-scientist-should-know/415.

Rawat, Siddarath. 2017. "A/B Testing Guide." Website. VWO. July 14, 2017. https://vwo.com/ab-testing/.

Shamsan Saleh, Ahmed M. 2024. "Blockchain for Secure and Decentralized Artificial Intelligence in Cybersecurity: A Comprehensive Review." *Blockchain: Research and Applications*, February, 100193. https://doi.org/10.1016/j.bcra.2024.100193.

"Singapore's Approach to AI Governance." n.d. Personal Data Protection Commission. https://www.pdpc.gov.sg/Help-and-Resources/2020/01/Model-AI-Governance-Framework.

Swayne, Matt. 2024. "Supremacy Surprise: Speedy Supercomputer Surpasses

Sycamore." The Quantum Insider. July 4, 2024. https://thequantuminsider.com/2024/07/04/supremacy-surprise-speedy-supercomputer-surpasses-sycamore/.

Sweat-Digital. 2024. "Unleashing Power: Modern Warfare's Transformation with Drones and Tanks." January 28, 2024. https://www.sweat-digital.com/keywords-modern-warfare-unleashi/.

"Tech and Education: How Automation and AI Are Powering Learning in Singapore." 2023. GovTech Singapore. February 23, 2023. https://www.tech.gov.sg/media/technews/tech-and-education-how-automation-and-ai-is-powering-learning-in-singapore/.

TechAhead. 2024. "Revolutionizing Workouts: The Impact of AI in Fitness Today." Www.linkedin.com. 2024. https://www.linkedin.com/pulse/revolutionizing-workouts-impact-ai-fitness-today-techahead-cjycc.

Techasoft. n.d. "Supercharging Productivity: How AI Will Benefit Workers." https://www.techasoft.com/post/supercharging-productivity-how-ai-will-benefit-workers.

"The Convention on Certain Conventional Weapons." n.d. UN Office of Disarmament Affairs. https://disarmament.unoda.org/the-convention-on-certain-conventional-weapons/.

Trident Information Systems. 2024. "The Benefits of Using AI-Based Vision Inspection Software in Improving Product Quality." Www.linkedin.com. 2024. https://www.linkedin.com/pulse/benefits-using-ai-based-vision-inspection-geyuc/.

"Understanding Facial Recognition Technology: How It Works and Examples." 2024. Visionplatform. January 27, 2024. https://visionplatform.ai/facial-recognition-sofware/.

Viliavin, Roman. 2023. "Customer Support: Using AI Chatbots for Efficiency and Empathy." Forbes. July 18, 2023. https://www.forbes.com/sites/forbesbusinessdevelopmentcouncil/2023/07/18/customer-support-using-ai-chatbots-for-efficiency-and-empathy/.

Zivcic, Antonia. 2023. "What Is Web 3.0: A Beginner's Guide to the Decentralized Internet of the Future." TechyIce. September 16, 2023. https://techyice.com/what-is-web-3-0-a-beginners-guide-to-the-decentralized-internet-of-the-future/.

Made in the USA
Middletown, DE
29 January 2025

70538442R00091